# Love Poems for Butchers

VICTORIA YOUNG

Copyright © 2020 Victoria Young

All rights reserved. No part of this book may be used or reproduced in any manner whatsoever without written permission except in the case of brief quotations embodied in critical articles and reviews.

"How to Give a Passive Aggressive Handjob" first published in *PRISM International Magazine* Spring Issue 2016, and "How to Have a Fake Affair with a Real Celebrity" first published in *Cream City Review* Spring & Summer 2017

ISBN: 979-8-68-384875-0

Writer. Dater. Masturbator.

# CONTENTS

| | |
|---|---|
| Brown Paper Bag | 9 |
| How to Break Up | 24 |
| Garbage Men | 30 |
| A Date, Gynecologically Speaking | 51 |
| Heart Like an IKEA Futon | 75 |
| A Series of Men Lying About Inches | 88 |
| How to Have a Fake Affair with a Real Celebrity | 104 |
| Fitness Tips for Mountain Lions | 129 |
| How to Give a Passive Aggressive Handjob | 154 |
| Fucking Like a Workout Plan | 174 |
| Perceived Online Slights | 188 |

# PREFACE

Tell the story of that time you fucked a man and then he stole your video camera and cell phone. Tell everyone how you're tainted by all the slights of your past. Say it nonchalantly though, so they know you're not broken just different. Smile while you deliver the words into a microphone. Channel that poem about Frida Kahlo, about the woman with a heart like a four-poster bed. Don't let them see that your heart is an IKEA futon. You've already bent in the middle under all this weight. Tell them that men are monsters and laugh—everyone knows you're joking. You're joking right? Just a little hyperbole. Tell them about all the men who treat you like a walking vagina, a doll that talks, a toy to fuck. They will tell you that it's dating. They will blame the medium, the mode, the method of contact, the context. Anything to set men free. Anything to explain away the truth about monsters—that they had the location wrong your entire life. Under your bed is nothing but peaceful dust. The real terror is in your sheets. Case your pillows in hurt. Spend your entire life looking for a comforter that can do its job.

# BROWN PAPER BAG

The first time I touch a penis I am seventeen and in someone else's empty tent. There are no sleeping bags, no stretched-out foam mattresses. I can feel the hard dirt underneath the tarped bottom. My jacket stays on the whole time. We never even kiss.

He opened his pants in the darkness and felt for my hand. I immediately squeezed too hard, and it deflated to something like a pudding-filled balloon. He was an older boy from Chilliwack, a town of importance for no other reason than it wasn't my own. He was older and unknown, so the story goes. After he went soft, we sat in the tent in silence, until he told me that he was much more attractive to my friend.

The second time I touch a penis is right before putting it in my mouth. It was significantly smaller than I had expected. Like sucking on your finger to get a ring off—it was a tiny baby erection. His name was Errol.

"Like Errol Flynn," he said, and then he imitated a swashbuckler. He was just a boy from a group of boys, and I was just a girl in a group of girls, and we were all across the border watching the 4$^{th}$ of July fireworks. They looked the same age as us but weren't. We had just graduated the week before; they would be starting as seniors in September, seniors at a school in another city, a school that wasn't ours, a city that wasn't our own. They were foreign, which made them perfect.

"We have a cabin," they said and then lead the way.

I was crouching the second time I touched a penis. We had walked away from the group and secluded ourselves in the trees. We were kissing and then I was crouching with his tiny baby penis in my mouth. Only my second penis ever and it didn't hardly seem that bad. He had asked if I would, asked had I ever before.

"Want to suck my dick?"

I was offended. He had barely touched my boobs, and this seemed like skipping too far ahead, but I did want to see his dick. I wanted to see it and taste it and know things about it. I wanted to know what it was like to be the girl a guy wanted sucking his dick, even if it pinched a little knowing that maybe that was any girl. No one had ever asked me before. I sucked on it like a Twizzler and within a minute he came: thin and sweet. I swallowed without much thought. It went down with ease, much like I did, apparently.

The fourth time I touch a penis I am blackout drunk. Two girls find me lying on a cement bench, my back and arms sprawled into the bushes of a courtyard outside of the student union building. They call an ambulance. I vomit. My jeans are undone. It is unclear if my underwear has been off. I vomit. The paramedics show up and take me to the hospital. I have alcohol poisoning (not for the first time). I vomit.

"Luckily," they say, "We don't have to pump her stomach because she's bringing it up on her own."

"Luckily," they say, and then they call a woman from WAVAW (Women Against Violence Against Women). They do a rape kit, and I try to stop them.

"I have my period," I say clumsily. Drunk arms, heavy tongue, sloppy heart. I assume they've seen this a hundred times before.

"Still," someone says, "just in case."

I vomit.

They put my underwear with the maxi pad I was wearing in a large brown bag. I am seventeen and a late bloomer. My mother never really told me about tampons. I wear maxi pads because this is all I know. But I know enough to feel shame, to know that maxi pads are not sophisticated. I know enough to be ashamed that I am a woman whose body is a tragedy.

They fold everything up into a brown paper bag, a bag big enough for a week's worth of groceries, big enough to hold a baby. My sorrow will overflow it. Drunk, raped, or not raped, ashamed of being raped, or not raped, found with pants open, bleeding, *left her there just like that.* Not a bag in this world big enough.

The nurse pats the bag on the table beside my hospital bed. "Just in case you want to press charges." My head is an out of range radio. Press charges for what? Against who? But I remember who.

I remember his dark hair, his face too pretty, the noise all around me from the freshman BBQ, my favorite white sweatshirt—the one with the holes at the sleeves because my mother had bleached it so many times—tied around my waist. It happens in flashes, darkness against the setting sun. I'm falling down, and then his face, kissing, wanting to have sex. The sun dipping. Him holding my hand, me trailing behind him. And then me whispering in mild protest that I couldn't have sex because I had my period (and was a virgin and didn't know where we were). His smile, and then his British accent, which I would later find out was Australian.

"Just in case you want to press charges," says the nurse, patting that looming brown bag. I never would want to press charges. I never knew if there was anything to press charges for, though the police did come that night two weeks later when I saw him. I saw his face walking across the dance floor at the campus bar, and he told them that he didn't know me. They told me the next day at the police station having asked me to come in. They said he denied everything, though I wasn't clear what everything even was. I wasn't crying rape; I was just crying. But there was something in the way he lied that always stuck in my jaw like a punch, swallowed like a brick. Maybe he was just scared. I could relate.

They let you shower after collecting the rape kit. They gather up all the data and then hand you this bag, so that the decision is yours—whether or not it should be tested. They handed me a bag of granny panties and a used maxi pad and my dirty heart and then they let me take a shower.

The lady from WAVAW stayed with me all night. She waited while I tried to get clean, still drunk, in the weird little hospital shower that felt so tight around my shoulders. Beige enamel everything. It all blended together—I couldn't tell if it was the alcohol or if I had cried out my contact lenses. Even the air seemed out of focus. My clothes were covered in vomit. The lady from WAVAW brought me a denim shirt and the most ridiculous pair of banana-yellow sweatpants. I kept the pants for years, folded in a bottom drawer, their presence a necessary reminder of her kindness. A woman whose name I don't know who sat with me all night while I vomited and cried and was examined. She waited while I showered and brought clothes that would fit my chubby body. I wondered how deep she had to dig into the donation box to find those fat-girl garments.

When I was ready to leave the hospital with my puke-covered things and brown paper bag, we got in a taxi together and she took me back to my dorm. She offered to walk me to my room, but I didn't want to draw any attention. She understood. I never did press charges because I was never sure if there was anything to press charges for. I put the paper bag on my dorm room floor, climbed into bed, squeezed my eyes shut, and tried to sleep. I wondered about the girls who had found me in the courtyard. I tried to remember and not remember. Maybe I never even saw his penis. My eighteenth birthday came two days later. I tried to think about cake and keeping down the morning after pill they said I should take "just in case."

The fifth time I touch a penis I am eighteen with a thirty-year old man in my dorm room. The Internet is a thing now—chat rooms, and forums, and pre dating-site dating sites. This is where I "meet" Todd—a thirty-year old actor slash UFC fighter (before UFC is really a thing). He has spiky blond hair and looks like he would have auditioned for The Real World, had they had a late '90s Vancouver season. He's wearing a thick white dress shirt and mom jeans in a photo that looks like it was taken in a Sears studio. But he's older. I repeat it over and over in my head. I know it in my bones; I matter more because he's older. Older men love fat girls who don't yet love themselves. We chat on and off for a week.

I am busy pretending what happened in September didn't happen, whether or not there was anything to pretend not to have happened. I drink too much and am having a great time in University. I rarely attend class and do moderately okay. I write an essay on a book I've never read and get a B+. University, it seems, is exactly like high school—I'm skating by and still haven't learned how to try or work hard. I am too afraid to care about anything. Sometimes I eat way too much; sometimes I stop eating entirely. For three days, I drink nothing but watered-down iced tea and stare at the flatness of my stomach in the mirror. I lie down to watch it hollow. Then, in an instant, I lose control and swipe my meal card like a rich girl with a Visa.

Todd sends a message to ask me about meeting up and we decide he'll come over on Wednesday night. Part of me thinks that his age makes him more desirable. The other part of me knows that this is embarrassing and shameful (which is why I tell no one). It doesn't hit me till much later that it's horrifying that a thirty-year old man would agree to meet an eighteen-year old girl late at night, that he would go to her dorm room, and that he's okay with taking her virginity the first time they meet.

On Monday, I chicken out (or, come to my senses). I feel a compulsion to tell someone, to have a second party agree that this is a horrible idea and not as wildly fun as I had originally hoped. Sitting in the cafeteria with a friend I let it slip and it all seems so scary and just *not right*. I (mostly, probably, almost definitely) decide that I'll message Todd and call it off. I give myself until Wednesday morning to change my mind back. After all, virginity is just an arbitrary construct used to control women, right?

Tuesday night I go out dancing with friends. It's more fun than I've had in weeks. We laugh, we dance, and we drink the exact right amount. After the club, we run across the street, arms linked in shrieks of friendship. We eat ninety-nine-cent pizza on a bench. We take the bus back to campus and walk home filled with joy.

Back in my dorm room, my ears still fuzzy from the drinks and the music, I change into an overpriced pink sweatshirt I bought to look cute and my grandpa's hand-me-down pajama bottoms with the stretched-out waistband. There is a knock at the door, and I answer expecting to see one of my friends too wide awake to sleep or coming to see if I want to watch T.V. in the lounge. But there he is, Todd, a thirty-year-old man, standing in my doorway on the wrong night—a lion in Sears clothing. He has a leather backpack, which I imagine must be full of condoms and candles and whatever else people need when they have sex (or, commit murder). I fumble with my words. He looms in the doorway. I don't want anyone to see him, so I rush him inside. I wonder how he got in the building, who let him in at this hour, who didn't notice how old he was? I don't know what to say.

Standing in ratty pajamas, my sweaty hair up in a ponytail, I tell him that he is here on the wrong night, that the plan was to meet tomorrow, that I was going to cancel, that I wasn't sure.

He says, "We can just talk."

I motion for him to sit on my frameless twin bed, on one half of the two-person dorm room that I have to myself. I motion to this thirty-year-old man to sit on my twin size bed, in my college dorm room, only a few months after turning eighteen, on the wrong night, making all the wrong decisions, and he does.

We hadn't been talking for long when he asks if he could kiss me.

"I might have bad breath."

It's the only thing I could think of to make things stop, to slow things down.

He reaches into his backpack, brings out a pack of gum, and hands me a piece. I was pulling the ripcord, but my parachute wouldn't open. Maybe he would catch me. If I let him kiss me, I thought, maybe it would be fun. Yeah, maybe this would be great. And so, I let him kiss me. It all followed pretty quickly after that. He went slowly, but it still hurt. It didn't feel great, not even good, really. It felt very precise and quiet. My legs bent; knees pointed at my ears. I thought it was funny that fucking and giving birth were in similar positions (which shouldn't have been funny at all given the obvious connection between the two). We kissed some, during; other times my left cheek was near his face while I looked at the cream-colored brick walls and never once worried that a neighboring dorm mate would hear me. It was much quieter than in the movies. I made some noises I thought were appropriate. I mostly just waited for it to be over, to be a grown up, to be a woman, to have been fucked, to have been attractive enough to be wanted.

    Afterward, we talked for a while, and I kept waiting to feel an attachment to him. He told me that he was from Nova Scotia, that he used to fight on rooftops because ultimate fighting was illegal. He wrote a phenomenally awful poem about equality on the back page of my journal. I think it had something about animals in it. He was older (I had to keep reminding myself that he was older). His desire, his dick, had given me a value that also made my skin crawl. It was embarrassing and pressure filled. Outside of my weakness, he had made me feel wanted. Still, even at eighteen I had a feeling that his desire was worthless, that the way men viewed me was pathetic and inhumane.

    The following week, he came back again. This time wearing jorts. I tried not to laugh when he told me that he was allergic to condoms, as if latex was the only kind they made, as if I didn't know any better, as if I was an idiot. I told him condoms were non-negotiable, and when he suggested I just suck his dick instead, I stood up a little taller. The dumb things he said were fertilizer for my spine. When I laughed, just a little, and told him that he should go, he stormed out of my dorm room. He returned a few minutes later because he had forgotten his keys and, knocking so loudly and aggressively, managed to catch the attention of the large group of eighteen and nineteen-year-old girls craning their necks from the dorm-lounge to see the commotion. Todd left again in a huff, this time to a chorus of laughter from the lounge. I laughed along with my friends, but I was mortified that I had let this man's touch set a value on me.

I only ever saw Todd once after that. It was April and I had, "withdrawn from UBC for medical reasons," which is a polite way of saying I dropped out, but they understood because I was depressed. I was waiting at a bus stop downtown, when I saw him come flying by. He was running with a girl his own age to catch a different bus. He seemed happy. He never saw me.

# LOVE POEMS FOR BUTCHERS

# HOW TO BREAK UP

Ask him to get married. After years of long-distance love, the week after your twenty-eighth birthday, when he decides to buy instead of rent in Seattle, and you are locked into UBC for the next two to three years for another degree, tell him to make a choice.

Say: I'm going to send you an email.

Say: I'm tired of the distance; I'm tired of standing still; it's been almost six years.

Say: It's now or never.

He says, "Not now."

You say, "Then never."

Wash yourself in tears and then get over it.

When he gave the reasons for "not now," he said that he loved you but worried about your depression, your mood swings, the way it seemed like you had given up on losing weight. He loved you no matter what, he said, but he wanted you to live forever.

Hate absolutely everything about this love.

Stop talking to your friends and avoid, where possible, telling anyone what's going on. If you isolate yourself, you can deny the end of the relationship. Drown with tight lips.

The first two weeks will be the most important. You must immediately try to lose as much weight as possible. Go back in time and start to diet sooner. Make him rue the day that he loved you enough to want the best for you. Lose an arm and a leg; lose your entire weight in gold; lose ten pounds. The loss will be a sign that he was wrong; you are worth it.

Now is the time to bargain away the ending. Set a trap for him. Ask him to drive up for Halloween. Buy a sexy costume. Envision the scenario where he sees you at a Halloween party, you kiss in public, make other people jealous with your connection, and find a way back to happiness. But he will not drive up from Seattle to Vancouver. He is sorry; he is miserable; he wants everything to be okay.

"I didn't know," he says, "that you were thinking we might get back together soon." Focus on the word "soon." Move it around with your tongue.

He didn't know that you had wanted him to come up for Halloween. He didn't know that you were trying to lose weight again. He didn't know that he had made you feel worthless. He didn't know, he says.

"But no," he says. You are not getting back together.

Skip past everything to acceptance.

"Fine," you say and ask him not to contact you anymore.

"Not at all?"

"Not at all."

Say: I need time and distance.

Say: This is going to require amputation.

Say: I will contact you again when I am whole.

Collapse in the hall on the way to the bathroom. Press your mouth towards the carpet, straining. At first, be silent as the carpet fibers tickle your lips. Then, wail. Push the sadness out from deep down. Use your diaphragm. Put your entire body into this grief. Feel wholly justified in this wallowing. People break up all the time. This is as clichéd as it gets, and in that you can find some comfort. Speak only to your parents. Ask if they miss him. Ask how to get over this. Tell them that you are filled to the brim with regret for having ever loved. Cry until you become thirsty.

You are regressing; this is depression. A week goes by and nothing changes. On the bus, in the middle of a lecture, while waiting in line at the supermarket, you audibly hiccup from a sharp remembrance. It becomes difficult to focus, but you must not let your life fall apart. Make an appointment to see a counselor.

She will ask you to describe how you feel. Show her. Hold up your hands, say it looks like this; gesture wildly, hands shaking. This is anger. She will be taken aback. She will ask what you are so angry about.

Say: He took my best years.

Say: I'm going to die alone.

Shake your red, angry hands in her tiny office.

Say: Who will love me now?

She will tell you that we all die alone. She will tell you that marriage is not a guarantee.

"Divorce happens all the time," she says. "People leave."

And that's when everything changes. Snap. Just like that.

*Just like that?*

Just like that. This is moving on. You broke up over Thanksgiving (the Canadian one), and by Christmas you are no longer broken. Put up a profile on Plenty of Fish. Start your new life. Go fish.

## LOVE POEMS FOR BUTCHERS

# GARBAGE MEN

All good first dates start with the basic fear that you'll be murdered. Or worse yet, that the other person will embarrass you in public. The first date I go on after the breakup of my six-year relationship looks more like a drug deal than romance.

He's a bartender named Stacey with black hair and the easy confidence of a straight white man. In his dating profile picture, he's leaning forward across the bar with a Cheshire grin. He looks straight through the camera and deep into my eyes, or perhaps maybe just at his own reflection in the lens (it's hard to say). The first time we plan to meet he flakes at the last minute by saying something about schedules and unavoidable things. He sends a text that says *sorry* and arrives far too long after the fact. I decide not to speak to him anymore. But he continues to text. He says *please*.

I say that I'm busy, super busy, just so goddamn busy, and then I watch TV and ignore his texts.

He says: I'm sorry

He says: I really want to meet you

He says: You seem so great

He says: I'm really sorry

He says: No pressure, we can just go for a drive or something without even a hint of awareness.

Only, I am not so busy. It's late, and I'm bored and awake. It's Christmas break, and I'm finished with exams, and I'm horny and should know better, but somehow, I don't yet know better. I'm twenty-eight and trying to date after a six-year relationship and a lifetime of believing men don't really want to date fat girls (with a few exceptions).

*Can you drive out here?* he asks, looking for unearned favors.

I know I shouldn't. I absolutely know this man doesn't deserve a second chance, doesn't deserve my effort nor my gas money. I absolutely know I will not fall in love with this man, but I'm not looking for love, I just want a couple fun dates maybe a cheeky make out—I just want some fun. I leave my parents' house and drive twenty minutes to the edge of Vancouver, where he lives. The city is covered in late night fog and I sit in my car and hold my breath.

*I'm here.*

The moment I see him I am filled with regret—he is wearing jogging pants. There is no bigger red flag than jogging pants. Jogging pants say, "I don't care what you think." Jogging pants say, "I am not here to impress you." They are a loudspeaker in my face. It's 1a.m., and we're both idiots but for very different reasons. He opens the door and gets in the car, and I realize his pictures are a lie. They are both *him* and *not him* at the same time. They are who he is on his best day, in black and white, from the best angle. His face is his face but not as good. It only gets worse from here. When he starts talking, I want to disappear.

His words are jerky and aggressive like a rabid animal, and I look for foam around his mouth. He's excited and frantic with no clue that I'm not having fun. As he sputters something about "new experiences," and "never having been with a big girl before," I want to vomit all over his stupid grey sweatpants. To him, I am something to be ordered off a menu and sampled—my size is a fetish. To him, I'm no longer human, even if he doesn't know he's doing this (which, of course, he doesn't). It sounds ugly when you say it but he's too much of a fool to ever really understand what he's doing and how damaging it is—less so to me, having experienced this type of fetishization for years, but to others who are yet unprepared for the brutality of this world. After all, just because something isn't intentional doesn't mean the cruelty won't chip away at you. I hold my breath and wait for a lull in his machine gun chatter.

I blink my eyelashes and smile demurely (because I've been punched by a man I've rejected before) and say, "It's late," and "I should probably get going."

When he moves to hug me, I jerk like a cornered animal, hunch my shoulders, form a barricade around my heart. I decide this doesn't count as a date.

The next time I go on a date I'm (under the impression that I'm) a better judge of character. He calls before asking me out. He asks before calling me.

I text back *sure*, and then press my shirt into my armpits to soak up the sweat. I'm sitting in the reading chair in my childhood bedroom with the walls so thin you can hear my heartbeat from the bathroom. I already have a bachelor's degree, but I'm living here so that I can afford the school that I've gone back to in order to earn another one. I'm switching careers and trying harder this time. Dating feels like I'm letting my parents down—fun without success is irresponsible. You are not allowed to be careless when you're indulging in your dreams. I try to keep my voice down. When he calls, we laugh, and I remember nothing about the call except our plan to meet for coffee.

When we meet at Starbucks, I try to look thin; try to think pretty thoughts; I wish myself to be just a little better than I am. He hugs me like hairspray: medium hold. We talk and laugh and tease each other and then go out for dinner.

When the bill comes, I offer to pay for half, and he blindly accepts. Disappointment courses through my veins. I want him to pay because women statistically make less, and as a student I make practically nothing. I want him to pay because it would mean that this date was worth all the makeup (which he would never feel a social pressure to wear) and the haircuts (which I would always have to pay quadruple for) and the underwire in my bra (which digs into my skin just to keep my breasts at the height men like and he would never have to endure). I want him to pay so that I could see his empathy, that he could lay it out for me, that it would show he understood what it had taken for this date to happen, that while he had just showered and showed up, I had spent hours getting ready to make this all possible. I want him to pay as if to say that he understood I had risked murder to meet him and that had to be worth at least $13.99 + tax. But I say nothing.

Back at his place, we watch the movie Hurt Locker because nothing screams romance quite like a violent film about the trauma of war. During the movie, he reaches out to hold my hand, which is sweet and endearing—an antidote to the violence of the movie and him having not paid for my meal earlier. Except, he moves past my hand and begins stroking my forearm with his fingers. It's neither sensual nor sweet but a bit like something you might do to a friend the first time they take drugs. He turns to me, his eyes wide with excitement.

"Do you like this?" he asks.

It tickles and the whole thing feels weird (even weirder now that he has verbalized it, practically begging for validation). Men truly have no idea what cornballs they are.

"Yeah, it's good," I say shrugging and turn my eyes back to the movie. The way he's drawing lines up my forearm feels extremely bizarre in its precision, like this is what someone had told him do rather than what genuinely feels good.

"It feels nice," I add to make up for lost ground, and then look up from the movie I've been pretending to watch to find him staring at me. He puckers his lips like a fish and moves towards me. We are only inches apart, but it takes forever for his lips to reach mine. I feel like

I'm underwater—uncertain which direction to swim, which way is up or down, fight or flight. But that's when the real surprise comes because he actually kisses wonderfully. The kisses get more intense and his chest presses against mine and we lean back together against the couch and I think maybe this is going to be great after all.

And that's when I feel it: wetness. My tampon is leaking. Here I am on a first date with a hot guy whose conversation is good, and though he kisses a bit like a fish and didn't pay for my dinner, I'm thinking I might like him just a little, at least enough to have some fun, and our lips and tongues are dancing and all I can think is that I'm going to bleed all over his couch like some kind of psychopath (or, a woman with her period). It becomes hard to focus on anything other than how every movement of our bodies is likely to widen the leak springing from my vagina. I pull back from his increasingly passionate kisses and politely say, "I have to go to the washroom." Smooth.

In the bathroom, I look in my purse for another tampon. I search every pocket frantically for a mighty shield of cotton to save me from this bloodbath, but there is none to be found. I sit down to pee and consider my options, none of which seem very good. I wipe what leakage I can while being careful not to dislodge my current tampon and pat the seeped blood from my underwear with toilet paper. My only saving grace is the fact that, in an effort to conceal my chubby belly, I'm wearing a homemade version of Spanx (which is really just a pair of leggings cut into shorts and hoisted up to my bra). Regardless, it acts as a second layer between my bloody mortification and the world. The second layer won't hold out forever though, and I can't very well come out of the bathroom only to immediately say I have to go—I'd look suspect for sure!

But all hope is not lost because like some kind of menstrual magician, I wrap toilet paper around the crotch of my underwear, creating a third protective, though flimsy, layer against my body's attempt to ruin this fairly okay first date. Doesn't my uterus know that he is tall with excellent hair? (I mean Jesus Christ, body, get it together!)

I'm basically in a mission impossible movie at this

point and there's absolutely a clock on things. I figure this makeshift pad will keep me safe for another fifteen minutes, maybe half an hour if we're lying down, which seems like an appropriate enough time to make my exit. Half an hour is long enough that it doesn't seem, like I just clogged his toilet with a huge shit or something, but also soon enough that I don't leave a murder scene on the back of my dress and his couch. At which point, I would have to murder him for sure in order to avoid being "that girl who bled all over the couch on a first date" (little known fact: this is the real reason they created the category of *justifiable* homicide).

Twenty minutes later, I make my lady-like excuses about it being late and having had "a great time," but, "I really must be going." He smiles as I put my sandals back on. I can feel the blood pooling as we hug goodbye, and he kisses me one last time before I walk off into the night and back to my car stain free.

The next morning, I wake up to find a text message from him *I had a great time last night.*

I'm ecstatic. *Me too.*

And then I wait for him to keep the conversation going. I wait for him to ask me questions or tell me interesting things. I wait for him to ask me out again. I wait. And I wait. And I wait. Minutes go by. Hours go by. Time ticks by like a clock covered in molasses. Time stretches out before me like an endless horizon while I'm busy pretending to be relaxed, nonchalant—breezy. Four days later, having heard absolutely nothing from this man who was previously contacting me daily, and had said the actual words (albeit in text form) that he had enjoyed our time together, I texted like a goddamn fool.

*How are things?*

*Good but I'm getting sick.*

I call instead of texting a response, which seems absolutely bananas now but was still very much a product of the time. He had previously told me that he was a phone-talker; he had asked to call before our first date, we both still had flip phones for Christ sake; calling didn't seem that abnormal. Except, he doesn't answer. I had shown my cards and it felt like he could see right down to the very most embarrassing parts of me. This man, who had only just texted me, was now not answering his phone and it was like a slap in the face. Being the emotionally intelligent, aggressively mature, and experienced dater that I am, I take it all in stride.

Later that night, he texts:

*Sorry I was sleeping aka getting rest, maybe we can hang out on Friday? I'll let you know how I feel*

I, of course, do the only adult thing I can think of and don't respond.

Two days later, I get a text from him that reads:

*ltrkl)))shfsdd8\*\*&^&^pdjhfl&a#$#I+=13*

It's basically a love poem.

*Are you sitting on your phone?*

*No lol! Telus doesn't play well with other phone carriers, this is what I said – Hey! It hurts to talk, I'm back at Dr. not feeling any better. Hope your enjoying sunshine ttyl.*

I respond and we have flirty banter (I'm not a heartless monster, after all).

Two days later, I get another text from him.

*Hey! So are you wanting to get together tomorrow night? Maybe you can come over to my place, that would be nice, hopefully I'll be feeling 100%.*

*Yeah that works*

But I'm not entirely sure it does. I don't like his use of the word hopefully. Then again, who am I not to trust a man to be an accurate observer of his own health? (Spoiler alert: I would be a smart woman not to trust a man to be an accurate observer of his own health). Friday afternoon, I text:

*Hey Cutie! How's my favorite patient?* (Jesus, I'm adorable)

He texts back: *Just at Dr.'s again*

I text: *Because you're still feeling sick? or to get the go-ahead a.k.a. not contagious?*

No response. Two hours pass.

I text him again: *You still at the Dr.?*

The silence is deafening, a lonely mountain echo. You could hear a pin drop the silence is so intense. Children in far off lands are telling the story of the lady who thought she had gone spontaneously deaf (except that it's so quiet I can actually hear them telling each other the story). The next morning, I get a text from him.

*Sorry fell asleep after I got home. I ttyl when I feel better*

*Sure. Feel better* (passive aggressive as fuck).

What I was actually thinking was: Are you fucking kidding me? Why hadn't he just texted somewhere between the doctor's office and his, apparent, sudden onset of narcolepsy? I would've felt more pity for his bout with the plague had he taken even a second to send a text message, something akin to: *I'm dying, go on without me.* And then he would've remained in my good graces. As it stood now, I wasn't sure whether or not I still even wanted a second date (assuming he ever asked for one).

But *you*'d be surprised how quickly a person can forget things that are displeasing: pain, disappointment, fish puckers, inconsiderate men. And, how easy it is to remember the good stuff: tall, butterflies, possibility for hot sex with a man with good hair. So, when he got over the cold a week later, and called to see if I wanted to hang out, while still having reservations about the whole thing, I agreed to go. The truth is, I was still pretty excited to hang out (read: absolutely fucking bored senseless and willing to settle for a fun night or a fun story). That was until he told me that he was having dinner with his mom and could we meet after at his place to watch a movie? In a heartbeat, I'd gone from excited optimist to weary dupe. He had asked me to hang out and I had foolishly agreed before hearing the terms. No dinner, no effort, just a movie at his place. Plus, what kind of monster double-books their own mom?!?

But I had already said yes. So, when Friday rolled around, I went to his place.

Standing in the orange glow of the outdoor lighting above his side-door, basement suite, I am optimistic and full of hope. And then he opens the door wearing jogging pants, and I immediately want to cry. Nobody ever wrote a love poem about jogging pants. Sweatpants. Loungers. A tracksuit. Joggers. I can't help but wonder if he's free-balling in there. And before you get defensive, he is not wearing the stylish tapered kind. He is wearing the baggy grey sweatpants of a high school P.E./math teacher who absolutely should not be wearing jogging pants. Apparently, this was what a second date looks like. Why the fuck does this keep happening to me?!

I go inside anyway. His face, the one that still makes him look like the guy from that vampire show, is a siren call. He's got that chiseled-jaw-soft-hair-hot-dude-thing happening again, which immediately helps me forget that he's a garbage man, not that there's anything wrong with that, wearing jogging pants, which has everything wrong with it. We sit on the couch and talk while a hockey game plays in the background. He tells me about his brother. He tells me he wishes he could travel more. He tells me how many garbage men drink on the job.

"Do you?" I ask.

"No," he says, pausing to crinkle his face. "I could really kill someone. If a garbage truck runs into you, you're dead." He's silent for a moment and then says it again, this time more deliberately, "Dead."

His response is abrupt and catches me off guard. A bit intense for a second date, but I try not to let it bother me. I try not to think about all the drunken garbage men out there. We sit on his couch for the next two hours talking and watching the Olympics, which are local and fill us with nationalism, which is a lesser-known aphrodisiac: oysters, chocolate, pride in your countrymen's athletic prowess. Shortly after a local guy from Whistler wins the Gold in Skeleton and drinks a pitcher of beer while celebrating in the streets, he kisses me again. It's as good as I remembered and this time I'm not slowly bleeding to death.

Soon, we move to the bedroom and things are going swimmingly (that's a little fish call back for you comedy fans out there). Things are going so well that I feel it's only fair to let him in on the fact that this would not be leading to sex, at least not tonight. I would prefer not to actually verbalize this but when he pulls his dick out himself, I realize I'm going to have to say the actual words. He lets go of the ass cheek he had been grabbing; the disappointment, palpable. We lay in silence for several awkward minutes before he speaks.

"Bison," he says, his dick still hard.

"What?"

"It's the leanest of all the meats." He rolls over onto his side and props his head up on his arm. I had been thinking about kissing and fucking and he had apparently been thinking about meat.

"I make it for my lunch."

"Oh yeah?" I say, feigning interest, uncertain as to whether this is a diet tip or recipe. (Also, because what the fuck is he even talking about?!)

"Yeah, I just cook up some vegetables and rice with it the night before and put it in the fridge. Then, in the morning, I put it on the dashboard of the truck and by lunchtime it's reheated."

He looks at me expectantly. His eyebrows arch as if to say that I should be impressed by his ingenuity. I can't help but wonder if there's a bout of food poisoning in his future. My pants are still unzipped, but I'm fairly certain it's time to exit.

The next three weeks are a maze of declarations of interest (on his part) and plans that never quite materialize for reasons that seem highly surmountable: he had problems with his phone, he had problems with his job, he had problems with his life. One day he sends a text that simply reads: *H*. I call to tell him that his cell phone is still not working, but he doesn't answer. He texts to tell me that he's cooking dinner,

*Can I call you after?*

*Sure.* My eyes roll back into my head.

He calls and says more than enough words to explain something away without ever explaining anything away. Now though, I am busy with school and writing papers and soon exams. I no longer have time for men who are garbage, to say nothing of men whose business is garbage. I'm not even totally sure who is being kicked to the curb. All I know is that I am no longer so eager to give away my time. He tells me that his birthday is the day after my last exam. "We can celebrate then," he says.

"Sure," I say and think, maybe, but I doubt it.

He texts once a week for the next four weeks, *just to check in*, and I find it endearing but not actionable. When my exams are over, and I've finished my first year of my second BA, I text him to make plans, but we never make plans. He is as big of a flake as he was months ago when this all started. In one of his final texts, he asks how much time I would want to spend together, should we continue dating.

*Like, hypothetically?* He texts, as if I was asking for a committed boyfriend rather than someone with the ability to make a third date.

We never go out again.

# LOVE POEMS FOR BUTCHERS

# A DATE, GYNECOLOGICALLY SPEAKING

The summer before I turn thirty, I sweat until I can no longer tell the difference between perspiration and tears. I know my own worth intrinsically, though my body is a foreign geography and diet culture still resides there. I post before-and-afters on my Instagram. I enjoy the praise when people see how *fit* I'm getting. I regularly settle for men unworthy of my time because I want to go on adventures and meet new and interesting people, and I don't have that much experience with dating (and I'm hungry for more), plus it's summer, and I'll have to go back to school in the fall, and honestly, it's pretty fun most of the time even when it's *not that fun*. So, the summer before I turn thirty, I date the Venn diagram of men that I'm interested in and those who are interested back in me until the part where the two circles overlap disappears.

That's when he sneaks in, during the lull.

The first time he asks me out is on Twitter.

He says: *In light of the fact that you're looking for a man, we should meet for coffee.*

I cringe at this message from top to bottom. His attraction is non-specific and undiscerning. At the time, I am blogging and tweeting anonymously. I don't yet believe that the world is ready for a fat, sex and dating blogger. It's not that I'm unwilling to reveal my identity (I do, often and in person) but I'm not ready to attach my career prospects to this part of my life, yet.

*In light of the fact that you're looking for a man.*

Reading his words, I practically gag over the implication that he is a man not a boy. It's corny as hell plus I've always thought it to be a pretty worthless distinction having little to do with character. It feels like asserting value in yourself based solely on the lack of value in others. As if to say, I am a good person because I no longer belong to that group of people who we've all deemed not as good. But value speaks for itself. You don't have to say you're funny if you're funny. Plus, all boys who do not die eventually become men. That is how time works. The distinction is arbitrary and relative and the fact that he doesn't know this is giant red flag (which I promptly bury in the sand, out of view and easily forgotten).

I leave his message unanswered. I'm willing to settle but I don't need this shit.

He continues to message telling me that he had found my dating profile on Plenty of Fish, which made me think him smart (the bar being unbearably low). I assume that he'd been able to find me using the notable qualities of my age and city (all discussed on my blog) and my body type (BBW—a term I would never purposely use but is foisted upon me with every dating profile or porn category). I am always disappointed but not surprised at how few men find this a doable task. It's even more devastating to think about how many find it doable and still can't be bothered. Google was literally invented for this shit (actually I have no idea why google was invented, I should probably google that someday). But even this minor positive wasn't without its hiccups because I found it weird that he hadn't just messaged me on the dating website. Why message me on Twitter, a place I remain anonymous and use mostly for lamenting the existence of men, rather than on a dating site where I am specifically looking for a man to go out with—like wearing pajamas to a business meeting.

I Google everyone I date, obviously. Some people think it's cheating; they want to get to know you from the moment you meet and not ruin the mystery by catching the highlights ahead of time. But, obviously, those people are stupid (hear me out). It's a bit like taking an exam and choosing not to study because you like "spontaneity and mystery." You're not carefree; you're ill-prepared. And so, there's a real charm in knowing that he reads the blog, or at the very least knows about its existence. Still, I am hesitant. Not so hesitant that we don't message back and forth but hesitant. When I express my concerns, he says:

*It may surprise you but I have been blogged about before (favorably I might add) in a very famous local sex and relationship blog.*

Barf. Everything about this seems wrong and the person who said it wildly unsuited for me. I take issue with the notion of a local sex and relationship blog being famous. How famous? And among whom? The sell is too hard. I can't tell which is worse, bragging about being in a famous blog or an unknown one? Or still worse than both, the knowledge that the kind of person who would brag about this is someone who enjoys my writing and/or my personality. I am gutted (the results are in; I am clearly a terrible person).

But maybe he has only skimmed my writing. Maybe this is a false-positive. There is still hope, and so I ask if he actually reads my blog.

He says: *I have read most of your blog but I skip over some stuff. I don't really need to read through your critiques of other people's profiles (since that doesn't apply to me).*

Before I can offer up the fact that the critiques are satire and not how-to tips, he continues:

*My rule's pretty simple: No names, no pictures, nothing that should in any way point back to me. I don't really care what people say about me except a blog is not a place for any of your love interests to find out what you REALLY think of them. In other words, just tell people what you think and then your blog is always just backing up what they already know… no surprises, right? That's the key (in my opinion) to avoid running into trouble with your blog and your dates. Posting pictures (even if they ARE doctored) is probably not a great idea, you could get yourself into trouble if some of the people you write about find out they're shown on the Interwebz. That's just my advice to you, do what you want with it…"*

I want to light it on fire. I want to unread it and go back to simpler times. But there is more. He continues:

*I am not actually looking for someone new if you can believe it, I am in the process of moving my stuff out of my ex's by Friday and I am cool if you are not that into me. But, to hear you talk, I suspect I have a lot of the qualities you are looking for so there you go!*

Ugh. Can you even imagine being a person like this, someone messy and complicated with the audacity to be so goddamn confident?! I tell him the truth, in a kinder and more diplomatic way. I reiterate the weirdness (his); I highlight how uncomfortable it would make me. I say anything but the truth, which is that he seems like a pretentious dick, and I'm not sad enough for him, yet. I try to lighten the mood with hyperbole, but the effort falls flat.

I say: *I hope it doesn't tear you apart inside ;)*

I say: *I hope you can withstand the tragedy of it ;)*

I winky face my ass off.

He says: *I'm not torn up at all.*

I roll my eyes for days.

A week later, he messages again. This time, he asks for advice. He calls me an expert and, given how much advice I feel he needs, I can't help myself and get involved. I give him my email. I was under the impression he wanted dating advice and a woman's perspective, but the more we talk, it seems like he just wants to brag in the grossest way. He tells me his tale of relationship woes from getting married too young (and then divorced), to meeting a girl online (with whom he had *super amazing sexual chemistry, the kind you can't say no to*) and then had a kid with and, though they had been on and off again, had now realized they were better apart. I keep waiting to read the part about what kind of advice he wants.

He tells me that he needs sex. He says that he hasn't had it in so long (what appears to be only a few months) that he's become obsessed with it. He says:

*I am so obsessed I'm getting bitchy.* And then adds: *And moving into my new place means I have very little time for relationships, and work's busy, and so on and so forth.*

I have a special hatred for men who complain about being busy. It's such a cop out and there is never a time I wouldn't rather hear them say, "I simply don't like you enough," because then you can move on. Men who say they're busy are assholes. Unless you're the president, you're not that busy. Do us all a favor and cut the shit.

Finally, though, when I think I can tolerate him no longer, a question comes. He wants to know how long he should wait before having sex again, which seems a tad endearing on the surface, to be so concerned about politeness and kindness, but it turns out that's not at all the case. He rambles on:

*I have some standing offers from my exes and some considerable interest from someone new, but (and this may sound egotistical) I don't necessarily want someone vanilla. See, with my baby-mama ex (and another, nympho ex) I got to do a ton of shit that was new to me and I don't wanna give up the opportunity to do more of that. Like group sex, or exhibitionism, and whatnot.*

He wants to know if he should: *go for broke and date like a madman, or bide my time and see how things play out with the women I already know?*

I want to know what it must be like to be this kind of person, to be so grossly arrogant (and corny), to have so many undeserved options and be given so many possibilities, to be so utterly fucking unaware of what an asshole you (are) sound like. For a moment, I wonder if I am anything like him and if that were true, then it would seem that he, like me, simply doesn't know. I dismiss this thought before the weeping begins—I am obviously very humble and adorable. I must help this man, and in turn help these women. But, selfishly, it is a bit more than that—I have an unhealthy curiosity. There is a perverse interest brewing in me. What could these women possibly see in him?

My fingers fly on the keyboard until it sings. I tell him to get his shit together, to download some porn and buy some lotion and sort his stuff out because his life is more tangled than a toddler with gum in his hair. I suggest working on things with his kid's mother (I say mother because I can't bring myself to say baby mama) and that if all the standing offers are with ex-girlfriends and his desires no more substantial than getting this dick wet, he might want to start cutting some ties and moving forward. I tell him that he's a grownup, and he should quit being so messy with everything. I also tell him that I don't think he's looking for dating even though he uses the word date, and that it's very simple to just ask people for what you want. When you want apples, you say apples. When you want oranges, you say oranges. Using coded language wastes everyone's time and (usually) ends up causing a lot of frustration and disappointment. Again, I reiterate that he is a grownup (and in total control of his own life).

The week drags on. The blisters on the back of my heels from working out refuse to heal and my weight refuses to go down. The man I went out with two weeks ago has not fallen madly in love with me. We had had a fun night and that was all I had expected going in. Still though, there is a sting when they do not so easily fall for me. There is a pinch when the men who have kissed my lips and laughed at my jokes do not call for a second date. Even if it's because they don't have their own place. Even if it's because they're moving out town for a few months. It all just sounds like disinterest and to be completely honest, it's hard to bear the burden of being so unlusted-for.

And so, in the lull, he gets in.

I tweet something about needing a pep talk. I am emotionally topless on the internet; my vulnerability hanging out for all to see. I am pathetic and this display is an overshare, but I can't help myself—I am flailing. He messages almost immediately. He asks what's wrong.

He says: *Cupcake*, which I don't know if I find endearing because it's a pet-name or because I like dessert.

He says: *Tell me what's going on.*

Since we're not going to go out, and because he'd already massively overshared, I figure what could it hurt and tell him everything. I tell him what had happened with the most-recent-guy, and about the weight loss, and about the pressure-filled loneliness of the summer of dating and the drought I find myself in. He is empathetic.

He says: *I want to go out with you, blog or no…let's go for coffee or something and see where it goes.*

I say: *okay.*

The night of our date, it rains. We meet in a bar in New Westminster. Sitting in a booth, side by side, we order drinks while MMA highlights play on the big screens, and he says, "You look beautiful."

He is tall with spikey blond hair and silver framed glasses. His face is angular although his body has a roundness to it, which is only worth noting because his pictures hadn't reflected that. He is dressed business casual and sitting too close for comfort. While his gaze wanders up and down my body and his belly presses against the table, I think about what it must be like to be a white man, to not have your confidence intricately linked to your physical appearance. I am uncomfortably jealous. Life feels like a gift for him.

"So, what makes you worth my time?"

I'm trying to be cheeky, but I worry it comes across as bitchy. He doesn't miss a beat and begins to recite his life resume: the job he holds, the things he owns. He seems like the kind of guy who sends food back too often and questions the oakiness of wine. I wouldn't be surprised if he said "m'lady" at some point. And yet, something in me wants to stay and get to know him better. It's probably the same part of me that keeps repeating loudly in my head *beggars can't be choosers*. Not to mention that I'm absolutely dying to know what all those women he had bragged about could possibly see in him.

"Take off your sweater." He gestures at the zipper on my black sweatshirt.

"I'm okay," I shrug.

"Come on," he says, "I want to see what you're

wearing underneath."

He probably thinks he's being flirty. I'm trying to pass myself off as someone fun and breezy, a real swell time, a great gal. And so, against my own sense of comfort, I do. He smiles in approval, but it doesn't really feel like a compliment. When the waitress brings our drinks, he reaches out to my necklace, which has dipped into my cleavage, and scooping his hand underneath the chains and drawing them out slowly, places them down on the outside of my shirt. Grossly intimate and forward, the gesture puts me on edge. I wonder what it must be like to be so unburdened by the rules of social decorum and decency. Again, I am jealous (and uncomfortable).

Knowing that he worked in human resources, I had already assumed he would be a great conversationalist, and he never lets me down. He sits too close and he touches me too much, but he never lets the conversation falter. Which is not to say that it's witty or interesting, but it's continuous, and I am always at the center. He asks a hundred questions and strokes my ego like a puppy. The intimacy is forced but working.

Everything he says is meant to be a compliment. He asks if I have many male friends and when I say, "No, I have almost none," he is not surprised.

"Of course not," he says, "Your sexuality is overwhelming."

This is not true, of course. To him, I am a blank wall, and this is all just a projection. Still though, it's kind of nice hearing your flaws spun into positive attributes.

When he brings up his ex, I am disappointed but not surprised. I drink my drink with intention. I let my eyes purposefully wander while he rambles. I'm employing so many clichéd techniques to alert someone to your boredom that I have to stifle my own laughter. When he suggests we go shoot some pool, I agree because at the very least it'll put an end to this conversation, which is actually more of a monologue, about his ex.

I am absolutely and completely wrong. As soon as we start playing pool, the conversation picks right back up where it had left off.

"Things are just really undecided at the moment," he confesses, and I almost start to doubt whether or not we are even on a date.

I keep waiting for all the great aspects of his personality, the ones that have instilled such a massive sense of confidence in him and caused all these women to want him, to present themselves. I know it's mean and uncouth to say this, but I am waiting for all the things that would allow someone who isn't good looking and doesn't have a good physique, and whose personality is mildly irritating on a good day and absolute shit on most, to have such mind-boggling confidence. I am waiting to find out what the fuck I'm so jealous of.

The first time he loses at pool, I see him wince, and it's the only time I'm surprised by him. He scoffs at my good fortune.

"Pure luck," he says.

The smile on his face should've been effortless, but instead it looks strained. When he demands a rematch, I comply. He wins the second game and while reveling in his glory, pulls me in for a kiss. I don't understand my attraction to him but still give in easily. Regardless of what my brain is telling me, my vagina is ready to roll.

After his win, I'm able to convince myself that his original lack of sportsmanship was a fluke, just a bit of nerves, or maybe his ego getting the best of him. But then we play a third game, and when I win again, he pouts like a toddler. The whole sore loser thing is a real turn off but, as I'm sorting the balls back into the tray to be returned, I look up and catch him staring at me. He just stands there—one hand leaning on his pool cue, the other casually in his pocket—looking at me. His eyes hold my gaze until my face burns, and I wonder if confidence is contagious; attraction, simply a magic trick.

Back at his place, his apartment is a mixture of a kid's playthings and unpacked boxes.

"I just moved in last week," he explains, and which, of course, I already knew.

I don't mind the boxes so much as the child's toys, which seem like an awkward reminder that he has issues with his ex, issues which remain unresolved. But I don't have any delusions about wanting to date this man. His confidence is inexplicable and in that I am interested—purely for science, of course—but the dramatic entanglements don't need to be a concern. I can stop trying to be that fun breezy girl and actually just be her because I have nothing to lose.

We haven't been messing around long before shirts are being pulled off. I undo the top button of his jeans and then his zipper, reach my hand inside his boxer shorts and find out that there is still, in fact, something left to lose.

There's this thing that happens when you find yourself touching the world's smallest penis and it creates a war within yourself. Part of you wants to run away, to pull up your pants and say, nope, absolutely not, and then there's the other part of you that would be crushed if someone rejected you for a part of your body that you couldn't control (or even one you could). An inner turmoil between self-preservation and kindness. After all, who wants to be the girl who breaks the heart of someone who already has the shitty luck of being endowed with the world's smallest penis? Less than three inches. Hard (barely).

His confidence is now even further mystifying. Because while he was only marginally attractive before, and while I often make the case that dick size is virtually irrelevant, he has the swagger of a rock star or a President or a tall, white man in North America. And the truth is that dick size doesn't really matter to me. Only something like ten percent of women can orgasm through penetration alone, and I'm not one of them so what do I care. And yet, the fact that he was kind of a jerk in every aspect of life that I'd witnessed him in just seemed so totally incongruous. Already naked, and with nowhere to put this new information, I could hardly think straight.

When he puts the condom on himself, I fuck him anyway. I bite my lower lip and hope that his dick is like a sea-monkey and will triple in size once immersed in something wet. It absolutely does not.

"Get on top," he suggests.

"Let's just keep doing it like this," I mumble. I barely want to be fucking him; I certainly don't want to get on top and do all the work myself. I know it's mean, but in the moment, I kept thinking how it was total bullshit that a man with the world's smallest penis wasn't working harder to please me. After all the years I had spent trying to be an interesting person in case men didn't like that I was fat, and he was allowed to just be nothing but blind, unsubstantiated confidence? The fucking audacity!

"I can last longer if you're on top," he promises, totally unaware of the fact that this is not an upside for me. "Get on top," he urges again, and again.

With each urging, what was left of my sexual attraction disappears until I finally cave and think—fuck it let's just get this over already—and I get on top. In less than ten thrusts he is ready to cum (so much for lasting longer). Rightly assuming that this is way too soon for a grown man to be cumming, he tries to shimmy out from under me. I assume this means a position change and plan to say, "I'm done with this," because fuck him and fuck this, but that's not what happens.

Instead, he sits up, swings his legs over the side of the bed and cums into his hand. When he gets up to go to the bathroom to wash off his hand, I think about how weird it is that he pulled out just to take the condom off and cum into his own hand. When he returns from the bathroom, he crouches near the bed and runs his hands along the sheets, which is weird I guess but doesn't set off any immediate alarm bells. He walks around the bed looking on the floor and then grabs the quilt and shakes it out.

And that's when it dawns on me, as it had probably dawned on him only moments before.

"The condom came off," he says without even a hint of shame.

"What do you mean?"

"I think the condom is inside you," he announces nonchalantly.

He offers me some bullshit about all the thrusting and the movement and me being on top, "etcetera," but it seems more likely that his penis was so small that the condom probably didn't fit (plus all the thrusting and me on top). I watch him continue to look through the sheets and walk around the bed again looking for it on the floor before the horror starts to sink in.

I want to cry. I reach my fingers inside myself in a

frantic search to get this, now disgusting, foreign body out of me. My heart is racing. I'm ashamed and enraged. Helpless.

"I can't feel anything!" I say, my voice rising in hysterics. "You have to take me to the hospital." I'm not entirely sure why I think the hospital would require the both of us, and why I won't be able to drive there on my own. I do, however, know that I'm not going to show up at the emergency room, alone in these dire straits, without the World's Smallest Penis by my side for support. YOU DID THIS TO ME! I want to scream.

"Relax," he says. "I'll help you get it out. Lay back on the bed."

And that's how it happened for me. That one time in every woman's life when you're on your back, legs spread wide, holding your breath, with a man between your legs, and all you can think is that things have gone terribly, terribly wrong.

As luck would have it, he is able to get his hand somewhere up near my uterus (or, based on my understanding of basic anatomy, probably more like my cervix) and deftly maneuver his fingers to retrieve the lost treasure. With my legs in the air over his shoulders, and him crouching down on the bed, he pulls that rubber alien out (after at least a minute of precision searching) and takes it to the bathroom to throw out. If I hadn't felt the skin-crawling sensation of it being slithered out of me, I would've asked to see it, just to be sure—this was clearly not a man who could be trusted.

By the time he returns, I already have most of my clothes back on.

"Well, I hate to hit it and quit it," I joke awkwardly trying to relieve the tension, and then, no longer caring, add, "but, uh...I gotta go." He didn't seem too bothered by my quick departure, which is understandable—I was a glaring reminder of his inadequacies.

On the drive home, there is a moment when I start to feel bad. Perhaps I shouldn't have run out of there so quickly? What's the big deal about a condom lost inside you anyway? But then I flashed back to that moment when it felt like he was up to his elbows in my vagina, searching and digging, and I forgave myself for any slights I may have caused. And then I made a mental note to make an appointment for my annual PAP smear.

# HEART LIKE AN IKEA FUTON

There were apartments, and they were available, but I couldn't bring myself to want them. They asked for references but not a damage deposit. I was snotty and thought it was because there wasn't anything worth damaging, but then I read on a website that it was the law. I rolled my eyes at the cracked paint and the uneven floors, sighing heavily every time I read the words *newly renovated*, and wondered if something was getting lost in translation.

They asked for first and last month's rent, which seemed legitimate enough except the website had said that that was illegal too.

"We know," said the girl in the manager's office when I asked, adding, "but everyone does it here," and then she just carried on like that was a good enough answer, majority rule.

It was thirty-five degrees Celsius that first week in Montreal. I was unprepared for the humidity and the feeling that my parents might die while I was away. I had already taken too long to make something of myself. Getting a master's degree was starting to seem like a hobby, entirely worthless and just for my own pleasure—a bit like academic scrapbooking. I hadn't stopped sweating since my plane touched down. The day my parents had to cosign my lease via fax, I texted promises of hard work. I reiterated that moving to Montreal to go to grad school would be worth it. I promised myself I wouldn't be just another fuck up.

My mother texted back: *Don't forget to have fun.*

The day I moved in, I came with two suitcases and a small backpack. I sat on the floor until my legs went numb, and then I made a chair out of folded clothes. There were too many hours in the day and nowhere comfortable to sit. My couch was my bed was my dinner table was my only chair was my only solace. The metal dug into my hamstrings every time I stood up. I scoured Craigslist daily in the hopes of buying furniture and avoiding murder.

I used to write all these stories about sex and dating, and I always put a lot of detail into describing just exactly how hot the men were because it had felt so much like a surprise. And it kind of was because I'd spent my whole life being told that fat people were unlovable and rarely get the kind of attention I wanted from men (until my mid-twenties and by then I was firmly in a committed relationship). So, when I started dating again after its demise, it did initially shock me—the sheer attractiveness of the men I was pulling. So much so that with this first man, in this brand-new city, I was hesitant to meet because he was just too good-looking. He sent me additional pictures at my request to help verify but with each new picture, model-posed and looking like a proper athletic wet dream, I was only more doubtful not less. Not one to leave things to chance though I asked for a final picture, this time holding up three fingers (because two seems like a plausible thing to be able to find if you were, in fact, using the pictures of a model to catfish). I didn't hold my breath, but then the picture showed up in my text messages just as I had asked and that was enough for me.

The night of our first date in Montreal, he kissed one cheek and then the other: the French way. He was exactly as gorgeous as his pictures had promised, but I didn't like the way he hugged me, his arms and body far too stiff. I'm still not sure if he smiled. I assumed he was somehow disappointed in my appearance though I did everything in my power to make sure my pictures always revealed me to be exactly as fat as I am. A lifetime of hearing straight men's greatest dating fear—that she might be fatter in person—had prepared me to always assume the worst.

However, I would soon find out that his standoffishness and general lack of smiling had absolutely nothing to do with me and everything to do with him. He didn't smile when we met because he was insecure about the gaps in his teeth.

"First thing I'll fix," he said, for the first time opening his mouth into a smile and gesturing at the gaps in his teeth, "once I have the money." As it turned out, men had their insecurities too.

After a short walk in the Montreal humidity, we perched on a brick ledge and I mentioned wanting to find myself a gym in the area. He gestured at my body and assured me that I didn't need to work out.

"Girls get too hard." He said it like a compliment, but I didn't like how easy men always found it to voice their opinions on our bodies.

It was ironic then that when, in an effort to make small talk, I asked about the tattoos on his arms and chest, and he refused to speak about them. He shook his head and smiled like he was keeping a fun secret.

Rumor has it that there is excitement in not knowing, but I'm not excited by silence. Mystery is for murderers, and people with nothing to say, the kind of people who text just to say: *I'm bored*, as if entertaining them wasn't a burden. It's exhausting to always have to write the story yourself, to be the one who keeps the conversation going, asks the questions, to be the only one with things to talk about. I looked again at his exposed forearms covered in stars and rows upon rows of musical notes and thought about the similarities between his skin and a Myspace page. Across his chest it read: *train like a freak*, and I couldn't help but think of all the ways we judged and then settled.

"Oh," is all I said.

People love asking the easiest question, and they love asking it even more when we're in the future, after it's all over—why did you go out with him then?

Because I was bored. Because I was fun and optimistic. Because I'm not a fortune-teller. Because at some point you have to realize that life is just a series of days held together by an arbitrary calendar system, and one day we're all going to die, and you may be remembered but you also might not be, so all there really is in this life are the handfuls of joy you can squeeze out of things in their exact moment. I went out with him because he was hot, and it was fun—I bragged like I had made him out of clay. I bragged because it was more fun that way. Finally, Montreal was shining with something other than my tears.

On our second date, he came over to my apartment and we made-out on my couch after pretending to watch a movie. Laying on my brand new (to me) shitty IKEA futon, I pushed him back just a little so I could look up at him—all muscle and chiseled features. In a move that felt sexy but quickly became hysterical, I ripped open the snaps on his blue gingham shirt to reveal what could only be described as the world's greatest abs—at least the best abs I'd ever seen in person, ever been able to run my fingers across, ever been able to feel pressed against my soft round belly. We kissed until the most uncomfortable black metal futon a hundred dollars could buy (used) bent and then broke under our weight, which shouldn't have been a surprise but was. I hoped he thought it broke because together we were too heavy—there was safety in numbers.

He had wanted to fuck that night in my apartment but had to leave for work as a bouncer (no surprise) and truth be told, I wanted to wait to fuck. People always offer counter-arguments to waiting like, "But we're all adults now so what's the point in waiting?" or "It's not like we're virgins," or "Wouldn't you want to know right away if the sex is good or bad?" as if any of these were the reason I liked to wait. The truth was I like to draw things out—there's something about the delicious about lusting over someone new—so much so, that I never want to end, and so I tend to make a concerted effort to sustain it. I had been on enough dates already that I didn't really expect it to work out long-term, so for now, in this moment of second date bliss, I wanted to stay home and masturbate to the fantasy of him while his kiss was still fresh on my lips. He would ask me out again; I was fairly certain. A man doesn't break your futon and your heart in the same week.

Our third date was a series of red flags I promptly ignored for all the usual reasons, paramount among which was that I had the time to waste. Men love to believe a woman showing interest has far more to do with them than what's going on in the woman's life, but in my experience that's rarely true. I've settled for any number of men and it rarely had anything to do with what they were doing or saying—in fact, usually my determination to go on second, third, and fourth dates was about how much time I had and whether or not I found them sexually attractive. The words they'd say were so often a thing I had to look past or ignore, rarely a thing that spurred my attraction on. So on this third date, I ducked past red flag (he hated his ex, had only just gotten her off his cellphone bill) after red flag (got so irritated waiting in the popcorn line at the concession that he dipped over to Tim Horton's and left me paying for my snacks alone) until we were safely in the silence of the movie theatre, at which point he, rather endearingly, reached out to hold my hand for the duration of the film. When we returned to my apartment, it wasn't long before my guy realized he didn't have any condoms and neither did I, so I easily sent his ass packing until our next encounter.

On our fourth date, he fucked like a salsa dancer. Slow, slow, quick, quick. Slow, slow, quick, quick. He fucked like there was a mirror behind the headboard. Muscles flexing and body posing, he fucked me like I wasn't even there. A moment ago, we were laughing and swooning and then suddenly I wasn't sure he could even see me. We fucked on polka dotted sheets (because they were the cheapest), on a child sized double bed (because it was the cheapest), and it felt like I had been ripped off. Our bodies felt miles apart. Even when his lips were pressed against mine, even when his tongue was in my mouth, even when he was completely inside me, we were apart. He barely touched my breasts; he never touched my clit. I kept waiting for a moment to move his hand in the right way, to make a suggestion, but the way he fucked was liked a game of double dutch, and I couldn't find my moment to jump in. Every breath I took felt like an interruption. I turned over, facing away from him, and grabbed my vibrator out from under the pillow. He didn't notice until the distinct sound of vibration emerged from my thighs like a snitch. His pace slowed and I turned my head to look back at him.

"You don't mind, do you?" I asked sheepishly, but

what I meant to say was *don't you even fucking dare*. He tried to hide it but the reaction on his face was unmistakable displeasure, and I hated him for even having an opinion.

He smiled awkwardly, his hands still holding my hips.

"It's just for, ya know—" I stumbled.

He half nodded, and I looked away. He picked up speed and, with the help of my vibrator, it started to feel good. I almost came, but I couldn't get his awkward smile and half nod out of my head. His feeling weird made me feel weird.

After he came, he laid down beside me, and I couldn't tell if he was too close or too far away.

"Did you?" he asked, though it felt more like an accusation.

I lied, "Yes."

He repeated the words "inside" and "outside" trying to grasp the ungraspable nothing of the female orgasm, I guess. He asked over and over like an interrogation, but he wasn't asking to understand. And it wasn't an issue of a language. He wanted to know what must obviously be wrong with me. I thought about all the women who had of course lied to him before. I didn't blame them one bit.

We kissed goodnight like there would be another date, but there would not be another date. We texted back and forth briefly, but he didn't seem at all as interested as he had been in the previous weeks, and his lack of interest only served to lessen what little interest I'd had for him. There were many red flags that I could ignore but his actively being uncomfortable with giving myself pleasure (because he was incapable) was unforgivable. A week later, looking for closure and scientific (albeit anecdotal) insight into the demise of our brief romance, I texted and asked for the truth. I wasn't afraid of rejection, plus his lack of interest already conveyed rejection anyway so what harm was there in asking for precise closure? I no longer cared for his interest in me going forward but simply desired an accounting of his side of things. *Just the facts, sir.*

And that is exactly what he gave me.

The texts arrived in his broken English, but I understood his words plain as day—no translation needed.

He said: *You should let the man try first.* And then added: *Plus, you didn't suck my dick.*

# A SERIES OF MEN LYING ABOUT INCHES

You never think this is how things happen, but far too often this is exactly how things happen. You think that you are strong and certain and have bones made of cement, but you are a house made of matchsticks, a paper lantern.

It happens slow, like pulling taffy in the winter, except that it's summer and they don't like when you call it taffy. He says, "Come on," and that's how it happens, slow and prodding. Because he says it once, and then again, and then one more time — his words, prodding at you, a countertop corner in your ribs, a stick held against your neck. He says, "Come on," asking for an inch, an inch, an inch more, and that's when you realize that life is just a series of men lying about inches.

It's summer and you're sitting shotgun in a silver Corolla with sad, grey upholstery and it smells like making the best of things. It smells like something you wanted only an hour ago. It smells like sweat. It's summer and this is how it happens, slow and prodding and eventual because he asked, and asked, and asked, and you couldn't sidestep fast enough. Think about the people in the apartment building just outside the car door, think about the humidity, think about how you're suffocating because the air is off and the windows are shut and *how long has it been since you wanted things to go slower?* now that they can't go fast enough. This is how things happen.

"Don't stop," he says, his words another jab.

Picture yourself upstairs in your apartment, wearing something comfortable and looking for the next possibility, another few inches. Look for someone just a little less likely to disappoint you. This is how it happens, in the summer, in the heat, with the windows up and his breath on your skin. It happens slow and without notice: a smile, a date, a kiss, the two of you laughing and now his pants unzipped. This is how it happens in the summer, on a first date, in the city, in the front seat of a sad Corolla, with your hand on his dick and his face in the rear-view mirror.

We met through a friend. We met on Twitter. We met at a comedy club. It depends who's telling the story. It depends where you start the timeline. We met in Montreal. You could say that I orchestrated the whole thing. That I made it happen. That I arranged to make it happen. You could say it was meant to be.

His name was Dustin (except we all know that it wasn't). His name was the name his mother gave him, but we can't call him that here because we have to protect him. I had no idea butchers needed such safeguards — the knife never seems to slip in the right direction. In a writing workshop, they say right to my face, "Why don't you just stop dating?" No one asks why we let men be monsters. Why am I expected to live alone and sexless because there are not so many great men? Every man writes in the margins—you deserve better, you deserve someone great—but that's not how it works. Plus, every man assumes he himself is great and they so rarely are. The man who takes the shirtless selfie and the man who thinks himself wonderful for not being the kind of man who takes a shirtless selfie are not so different from each other. Neither looks at himself clearly in the mirror. They read a story about how things didn't work out and suggest I stop trying, as if the story had been a letter to an advice columnist, instead of just a tale about the time I took a risk and it didn't work out. Why am I asked to be a fortune teller, for my broken bones to justify ever having wanted to walk? They say there are no stupid questions, so I guess you could say I asked for it.

He was a comedian in Montreal and unlikely to be a murderer because I had found him through a friend on Facebook, which gave him a tangible quality I assumed would transfer to real life (and a trail of information for the police to follow if I was wrong). A couple of messages later and he was inviting me to watch him perform.

The night of the show I took a cab seven blocks to avoid showing up sweaty but still managed to arrive late. I spent two hours getting ready for the date and Dustin carpooled with a friend. After the show, he said, "I really want to hang out with you," and then he leaned in close, and I could hear everyone in the room breathing, "but I got a ride with my friend so I have to go home to get my car if you want to hang out more."

"How long will it take?"

"Thirty minutes?" he said.

"Fine."

It wasn't, but a bird in the hand or something. Sitting with some of the other comedians while I waited for Dustin to return, the headliner leaned forward heavily on the wooden table and said, "You know, you really are a very beautiful girl." He paused, and then added, "I'm married so I can say this." But I didn't know that marriage was such a protective barrier. I'm not sure whom this was supposed to make safe. I was already too tired of men trying to convince me I was beautiful as if I wasn't aware, as if my fatness precluded this notion. They had no idea how many other men, exactly like them, exactly as unaware, wanted to fuck me. Though I guess that didn't necessarily mean beauty, but then again that wasn't really what he had meant either.

When Dustin returned, he asked if I wanted to eat.

I said, "No, I guess not," and then, "would there even be anything open?" I wanted him to say yes. I wanted him to say, "Let's get you some food. Let's get you a meal." And when I declined, I wanted him to insist, to finally have pressure applied onto something that benefitted me. I wanted him to say, "I want to get to know you over the effort it takes to have a stranger make us food."

"Probably not," he said and drove us down to the pier in Old Port where we walked around until it rained.

Back in front of my apartment, we sat in his car, and I did not invite him up. We kissed until it happened, the way it always seems to happen.

The first time he asked like a mime, adjusting himself so subtly that, had I not already been familiar with the moves, I might not have noticed. He sat shifting in the driver's seat, his erection straining against his jeans, and I pretended not to see.

By the second time, it seemed like maybe he wasn't really asking. He took matters into his own hands and placed one of mine on his crotch, which wouldn't have been so bad if that was as far as it went (but that's never as far as it went). He took my hand and I rubbed him through his pants, having caved under the weight. When he removed his hand from mine, I stopped rubbing and brought my hand back up to his chest (which was where I had wanted it to be in the first place). He waited a few minutes and then moved my hand again with his. Again, I caved. Again, I rubbed.

The third time he asked, I couldn't even hear the question. Sitting in the front seat of his car (which turned out to be his mom's), he unzipped his own pants—he pulled out his own dick. Sitting in a car, in front of my apartment, I wanted to be the trope of the girl who had to work to be sexualized by men, whose first dates were always an 'if' not a 'when' scenario. The rumor is that it's about desire, but when he pulled his dick out, it seemed it had very little to do with me. I looked at his smiling face, and then his hard dick twitching at me. He wasn't worried about anything. He was calm as a sloth having pulled his dick out. I was filled with a quiet rage—his audacity, his assumptions, his (derisive air quotes) throbbing cock and the expectation that I was supposed to do something about it. He whipped it out and I could almost hear him saying, "Here, you take care of it," like a goddamn baby. Even the way he pressured was pathetic. They always ask why I didn't make him stop, why I didn't just leave. But why does no one ask why he pushed? They say there are over fifty words for snow in the Inuit languages. I know a hundred ways to say he made me carry the burden.

When he opened his pants and whipped it out, the zipper teeth were so close to his dick that I wondered if it hurt (I hoped it did). I hoped it felt tight, like the walls were closing in on him, pinching, like the sharp metal teeth might bite his dick off—a real hostage situation. He grabbed my hand and put it on his dick, never once thinking that if I had wanted to touch it, I would've pulled his dick out myself. I assumed he thought I didn't know how zippers worked. He moaned the second my skin was on his.

Having grown up a woman, I've always known the rules of who I'm supposed to be. I am supposed to be made of resolve (but agreeable like a lady) with veins full of venom (but not the kind that poisons—dangerous enough to inspire admiration not fear). I am told that craving attention is needy and wanting to be desired is worthless, and that I am going to have to be superhuman if I ever want to be viewed as human. I have learned that I can be a vixen, as long as I'm never touched, and I can be a star, as long as I never ask them to gaze upon me, and that one mistake will most often (read: always) be enough to cost a woman everything, unless she relocates and starts over. Most of all though, I know that as a woman I am never allowed to be bitter. And that men are allowed to be anything shy of violent (and even then, context is important). It's hard to keep it all straight, this person you're supposed to be, the things you have to balance on your back.

"You're so good at this," he said, and I was already

nostalgic for when he was making me wet instead of just making me. Amid the pressure to be strong and the pressure to be wanted, in the fog of a rushed sexual situation, he stroked my ego while I stroked his cock. I couldn't remember how to say the words, "I'm not into this. I'm not really feeling how this is going down right now, but maybe if you turn back into that guy you were thirty minutes ago, we could save this, we could pretend that we're both better people. We could pretend that you're not awful and I'm not weak." Instead I said nothing because I didn't want to say, "No." I wanted to say, "Not yet." My shoulders sagged under the desire to be wanted (and when ready, sexually satisfied), and the disbelief that this was even happening because this man had been someone (possibly) worthy only moments before. I pitched forward under the weight of having not known better because I'm always expected to have known better, to have seen men for who they are as if I had a crystal ball. Long before I ever really know them, I am supposed to see these men at their core, when the people in their lives—their family and friends—haven't a clue. I'm supposed to have known right from the start, to have been able to break the code of human psychology. I'm supposed to assume that all men are awful (and just want to fuck me) without ever (my god don't you dare!) assuming that all men are awful (and just want to fuck me).

Why couldn't he see that I didn't want this? Why didn't he think to look?

When I finally said, "No," it fell on deaf ears, which should've been enough to make me leave but wasn't. My bones are not made of cement. My desires are not so set in stone. I melt in high temperatures. I am not microwave safe.

He said, "Come on," in that whiny way that men say it, pathetic and aggressive and judgmental. And I did, because I wanted him to think I was hot and carefree and beautiful, and he was ruining it every second he existed. He gently reached for my hand, which had fallen away from his cock when I said I didn't want to anymore, and he brought it back. While he sat in the driver's seat panting, and I dispassionately rubbed his dick, I wondered if my shame would stick to the windows. I wondered if his mom would be able to tell that a woman had become less-than in her car, if you could see it on the upholstery: a jizz stain on the shoulder rest, my withered heart underneath the floor mat.

He said, "Are you glad you came out?" and I answered, "Yes," because that's what you say when you're pinned to the mat. I learned long ago that nobody likes a complainer. So, when he asked if I was glad that I had come out, I lied because I wasn't sure if I wanted us to be over yet. I said, "Yes," because he hadn't earned my honesty and maybe that's just what I say when someone has had his tongue in my mouth and made me laugh more than normal but still not nearly enough.

"Forgive me?" I asked for it from my reflection in the rear-view mirror (don't worry, he never heard it).

"Forgive me?" I asked for it because I had wanted him to fuck me, at some point, maybe.

"Forgive me." Maybe I never even said it, but it was there, I was asking for it because he had told ten jokes and I had laughed six times, which was five more than usual, and I was desperate.

My desperation was unclear and ill-defined. I was desperate to kiss men who were good at it, and have hot sex (like real hot sex, not the kind of hot sex you have in your twenties where it feels relatively good but you never actually get off and it's mostly just about validating your ego and being a washrag for men whose adoration you haven't yet realized is worthless). I was pleading to be wanted in any other way than apathetically, lazily, for no other reason than I was there, *whatevs*.

I needed the next man who held my breasts to be one that made me laugh. But sitting in his mom's car with my hand on his dick, I hadn't laughed in too long. It was a problem of physics or geometry; I'm not sure which. Something about spatial relations and the relative size of my bra and his capacity for empathy. I may have still been wearing my seatbelt. Even though that seems insane, to be so concerned with my own safety when we weren't even moving. But, with his dick out and my whispers unheard, it seemed a bit like I might be crushed, and I didn't want to have to worry about surviving a crash and having to reset my own bones while waiting for the ambulance. I'm not the kind of person anyone rescues—my shoulders are too wide for sympathy.

He pulled out his cock and that's how it happened. He pushed a little more, just one more inch, said, "Come on," and I teetered on the edge. It took less than twenty minutes to convince me to do something I hadn't wanted to do and for him to cum. And that's how it happened. When I had thought I was strong, spine made of something stolen. It happened slowly, like pulling taffy in the winter, except that it was summer, and no one seemed interested in what I wanted. He said, "Come on," and that's how it happened, sitting shotgun in a silver Corolla with sad, grey upholstery and me thinking about his mom. It was summer and that's how it happened, slow and prodding and eventual because I should've seen it coming, because somehow it still seemed like my fault, because he had unzipped and pulled his dick out, and I became just a little bit unhinged. And when it happened, I looked away and tried to save the moment from itself, just in case. I thought about the people in the apartment building just outside the car door, about the humidity, about how I was suffocating because the air was off and the windows were shut and *how long had it been since I wanted things to go slower?* now that they couldn't go fast enough. "Don't stop," he had said, his words poking at my ribs. That's how it happened, in the summer, in the heat, with the windows up and his breath on my skin. It happened slow and without notice. That's how it happened in the summer, on a first date, in the city, in the front seat of a sad Corolla, with my hand on his dick and his face in my rear-view mirror.

# HOW TO HAVE A FAKE AFFAIR WITH A REAL CELEBRITY

You will find him one day, on Twitter, and follow immediately because he makes you laugh. Doing so will be a thing that changes your life. He will be the *blankity blank* of the most popular *blah blah* show since *that one show, you know that one*, which you would probably watch if only you could afford a T.V.

*Like* a few of his tweets. If you're lucky, he will notice that you have 10,000 followers and maybe, just maybe, think that you are a Somebody. You are definitely not a Somebody—but, if you're lucky, he won't notice that. Your bio will be funny, and your avatar will have been chosen for maximum appeal (read: from above and looking thin), so you can rest assured that you did all you could to make this possible.

## Writer. Dater. Masturbator. Don't worry, my parents don't think I'm funny either.

He will follow you back, and when he does, take a screenshot immediately. He could realize that you're ridiculous and unfollow at any moment. Post the photo on Facebook. Text your parents and tell them. This is the most exciting thing to happen to you since getting into grad school (who are you kidding? This is the most exciting thing to happen to you ever). The first few times he stars your tweets, take a screenshot of that too. Do not take any chances while waiting for the other shoe to drop. Your friends will joke that you are a celebrity now. Remember that you are not a celebrity now.

On a Thursday in December, he will tweet about the hockey strike. You will star this tweet, and he will send you a private message.

He types: *Hockey strike sucks!!!*

Take your time responding. Be patient, doing so will make you seem busy (regardless of the fact that you actually are busy). You are busy with grad school and work and pretending you have a life that is more interesting than this. Be super witty, be incredibly suave and smart and super sophisticated. Use words like you are a goddamn Somebody.

You type: *I know, right?*

And you have never been more brilliant. A few seconds will pass before you decide it wasn't good enough and write something more elaborate.

You type up a creative scenario, a fool-proof plan, something about how the two of you should campaign elementary school children to write thousands of sad little letters detailing how badly this strike is affecting them. Nobody ever says no to sad children.

He responds: *Thanks for the faves.*

Ooph. Not great. Recede into the depths of your self-doubt. Over-think to the edge of madness. Did he not think the letter campaign was funny? It probably wasn't funny. Oh god, he's going to think you're an idiot. Jesus Christ GET A GRIP ON YOURSELF! You are spinning out. He's just a person. Settle down and respond.

You thank him for making you laugh; he thanks you for being cute. He says all the things you wish men, who live within bus fare of you, would say. He thinks you're sexy. He thinks you're funny. He appreciates that you're in grad school, as if to confirm that higher education isn't completely without value. It's all flirt and swoon until he drops this bomb.

He says: *and I'm married so we have to be sneaky which makes for sneaky flirting sexting.*

Whoa. Wait. What? He's married?!? Of course, he's married. This is the Internet. Why would he be talking to you unless he was married? He could be out somewhere talking to supermodels and gorgeous actresses. So yes, of course, he is married (he is 100% married); the question now is whether or not this will bother you enough to offset the excitement of him wanting to talk to you. Or more precisely, as his message indicates, wanting to sext with you. Everything is so exciting!

Except, ugh, he is married. You will need to find a way to push the notion of his wife away. Maybe you can convince yourself that you're doing her a favor, spicing up their sex life without him ever actually straying. Married people need that, don't they? This will be the moment when you realize that you are a horrible person and that this is some fucked up logic. Try not to get down on yourself. Lots of people are horrible. It's about time you joined the crowd.

When you respond, act surprised it turned out this way. Act above it all, like you knew this would never be more than just playing around with words. Never admit that you looked at the prices for flights to LA.

He will ask what they all ask: *what are you wearing?*

Try not to be disappointed at his first foray into sexting. You were expecting genius and that was a mistake. He is an executive type not a writer. Still though, his tweets are hilarious, so it's okay to be a little disappointed. Chin up, it won't all be bad. Somewhere down the road he will say things that seem like magic. He will act like a dreamboat should. A dreamboat who is married. And on the internet. And basically-a-celebrity. Living in L.A., and you are not in L.A.

The conversation progresses and there will come a time when you will ask how old he is. He will tell you that he is old; he will use exclamation points; he is forty-five. Try not to be hurt when he never asks how old you are. Take no more than one moment to wonder how old you look. He knows that you're in grad school but that doesn't mean much. You could be anywhere between twenty-three and a hundred. This will be one of the few times you hope you look your age. Thirty-two is okay for a forty-five-year-old to flirt with. Thirty-two is okay to have fake sex with a real celebrity. Hope that he doesn't think you're twenty-three as that would be gross. Well, grosser than being married and flirting with a strange girl on the Internet. Consider how many levels of gross there are. Consider the morality of grossness. Consider getting more sleep.

As the sexting progresses, you will realize that this is why the dialogue in movies and stories never sounds like real life—because real life is awful. Real men (and women) are cheesy. His words will be goofy; yours will always be half-missteps and embarrassing upon review. But in the moment, in real time, when you think about him typing them to you, they'll make your cheeks flush and your desire real. You may even squeal with glee a few times. There will be moments when you practically beam. This is what it's like when powerful men flirt with Nobodies. This is what it's like when he talks to you. This is how to have a fake affair with a real celebrity.

You ask: *what would you do if you were here?*

This is the moment of no return. This will be your one chance to turn back, to stop the things you know will happen, before they happen. You will not make that turn; you will charge on full steam ahead. When it's over, you'll be embarrassed, having touched yourself to the words of someone you've never met. But embarrassment is worthless. Let go of that guilt. Finish your final paper. Finish marking essays. Go home for Christmas.

Back home, go to Costco with your parents. While your Dad looks at motor oil and your Mom is in the aisle for books, tweet the following:

**My life won't be complete until at least one guy wrecks his car checkin me out. And I win a Nobel Prize.**

It won't be your best, but it has a certain humorous charm. Almost immediately he will retweet it. This basically-a-celebrity, who has amassed another 10,000 followers since you first discovered him a month ago, will retweet it to his 30,000 followers. This is the Internet. This isn't real. This is ridiculous. And yet, it's not. This *is* real. Not the swooning and lust you feel for him but the exposure: your words, your picture, your presence on his timeline. That is real. It's happening. Take a screenshot and burst from joy in the dish detergent aisle of the Costco near your hometown. This may be the most exciting thing that has ever happened to you. Savor every moment. This is probably as good as it gets.

Enjoy Christmas with your family, have a great New Year's Eve with your friends, and try not to hope (don't hope!) for more contact from him. Try not to be sad when his face doesn't show up after every tweet. Fly back to school after holiday break. Act normal. Continue to tweet things only you could find funny:

**I accidentally got it on with a Miami Dolphin once. Just kidding, it was on porpoise.**

And then,

**Whenever someone says, "press pause" during a**

**movie, I go over & slowly press my palms against theirs because I like word play…and bears.**

He will star these tweets; you are both comic geniuses. This will be your window to contact him without seeming over-eager.

Thank him for starring your tweets, say something witty like: *thanks for starring those tweets; I wasn't sure anyone would find them funny.*

He will respond: *I did!!*

His exclamation marks will feel like declarations of love. Logic has never been further away.

He will go on a business trip halfway around the world, a real whirlwind thing.

He will say: *scouting for locations.*

You will wonder if you can feel him shrugging. You will wonder about the semiotics of nonchalance. Your mother watches his show. When she calls to tell you that they are filming abroad, pretend this is new information. It will be easier than explaining. Sometimes she watches to see if they ever read one of your jokes on the air. But they will never read one of your jokes on the air. Honestly, you're not funny enough, but thoughts like that sting so keep them to yourself. Or, more accurately, push them down and pretend they don't exist. Eat them like nachos (or just eat nachos). Ask him how the trip is going. Try to be brilliant, make a joke about the time difference.

You will say: *Is future me as adorable as present me?*

He wants to LOL you all night. It happens again; across the world and the Internet and his marriage. It is winter and you are empty, and he is alone.

Again, he will ask: *what are you wearing?*

Describe it to him slow and thorough, leave no detail unclear: red lace panties, topless, clean, and ready to get dirty. He will tell you that he wishes he could see you. Tell him you're not ready for that, that you don't want to be rushed. Try not to wonder if he would like your ample figure were he to see it in real time and not in perfectly angled, internet-safe pictures. You've seen pictures of his wife. She is fit. She is lithe. You can see her collarbone in photos. The only person who has ever seen your collarbone is an x-ray technician, and he didn't seem particularly thrilled by it. But you are not his wife, and maybe he has a secret fetish for fat girls.

You say something, casually, about how if he has an iPhone, the two of you could video chat with Facetime. You will say this mostly as a brush-off, a way to say *not yet* about him seeing you too closely without having to explain why you might not want him to see you too closely. And then, just like that, he types out his phone number, like it's no big thing. Like he's not the *something big and important* to the most popular *blankity blank* in America. Like he's not a goddamn celebrity. Like he's not a goddamn *married* celebrity. He just types his number, like somehow you can be trusted. When you respond with shock, he worries and asks: *was that a mistake?* Assure him that it was not.

He tells you that you are trustworthy. He types out the words: *I trust you* and it will feel like he makes it so by saying it, that you are trustworthy because he has given you something worthy of trust. The very reason he will feel safe giving you his phone number, is probably the same reason he chose you in the first place. You are trustworthy (to an extent). After all, I imagine his wife wouldn't think you're so great. Best not think too deeply on that one.

You send a text to his number: *Hey...it's me*.

You wait. There is no response. A minute goes by. Two minutes go by. You double-check the number, triple check. It is the right number; it is the number he gave you. You send another message on Twitter.

He says: *Sorry*.

He was busy taking a picture of his dick for you.

Remember this moment in time—the one and only time you'll be amazed by a dick pic. It won't be the size or anything weird, but the way he took it. He will be lying down, the camera facing up towards his face: full dick exposure, full face exposure. You will wonder if he's drunk. You will wonder if he's an idiot. You will want to believe that he trusts you beyond reproach because of something he feels for you, that there is some realness to this thing you two are doing. You will want to believe that this fake affair could one day be a real affair, all because of a face in a dick pic. You shouldn't believe any of this. But you will and that belief will be the thing that makes sexting with him feel like the best sex you've ever had, at the time.

When it's over he will thank you.


He says: *Thanks for being there* like you did him a favor, like you were a necessary hurdle.


You are the proverbial shoulder to lean on of Internet fucking. Push this feeling down. You absolutely cannot say anything about this to him. You cannot reveal that you think this is anything more than words on a screen. But then he calls you baby, and you take what you can get. What else is there but to emoti-con him into thinking you're fine with everything?

You don't wonder whether or not he cares about you—it is clear he does not. You are not in a relationship; you are a practice wall. You know this, not-so-deep-down. Yet, here you are, in this pathetically shameful place. You would never sell yourself so short for a regular man. But he is not a regular man. The way you value his status feels like Lego pieces under your feet. In the mirror you check for a shrinking spine.

The next morning, he sends you a message on Twitter instead of sending a text. You are hurt but not surprised. He will not have saved your number in his phone. You are not a number worth saving. Maybe that's too harsh. You are not a number he can be caught having. Thinking about it this way will make it hurt less but increase your guilt. Repeat after me: he is married; he is married; he is married. Pretend he isn't married.

The message reads: *Please delete pics. Omg.*

You press him for details, wanting to know why. You know why, but you want him to say it. You want him to break the spell.

You ask: *How come? What has changed from last night?*

He responds: *Nothing!!!!!!*

And again his exclamation points feel like kisses, feel like assurances. His exclamation points don't feel nearly as empty as they should.

*Just makes me nervous cause you can see my face. That's. All.*

And that's how he types it. *That's. All.* His punctuation feels like a love poem. He's embarrassed and vulnerable and worried about assuring you. But his punctuation is not for lovers. His periods are afraid. His exclamations are hollow. He is a married celebrity in this Internet age. You should bear this in mind. You should prepare yourself.

He will have been right about you; you are trustworthy because you actually delete his pictures. You won't take screenshots; you won't save the files to your phone. You delete the photos like a good, trustworthy girl. Later, you will regret not saving a token.

A few weeks will go by and no messages get sent from either party. But still, he will star your tweets, and you will star his. Every star will feel like a secret message that should be reassuring but isn't. Your friends ask when you're going to be on the show. They are certain that you will be famous one day. Know that the mistress never gets a starring role. Though, if you think about it, you won't really be a mistress, having never actually fucked each other. You will wonder what is more pathetic: having a real-life affair with a Nobody or a fake affair with a Somebody? These thoughts are slightly insane and not at all uncommon. Keep this negativity to yourself. Nobody wants to hear the woes of the morally corrupt. Nobody wants to hear that you're sad about your fake affair.

**Trust me, I'm not the girl you're looking for. Unless this is your bike that I just stole. My bad.**

He stars this.

**I faked an orgasm while sexting. I'm what's wrong with the world.**

He stars this.

Send him a message. Try not to pander; try not to be pathetic. Make only a few awkward jokes. He will lift you up. But it will feel just a little too much like you begged for it. Like you're an annoyance. He retweets the next funny thing you tweet.

**How soon after starting a diet are you allowed to be a total bitch because I haven't had a carb in over 3 hours.**

And the one after that.

**Relationship Status: Mythical**

Two weeks pass and he retweets you again, but time has elapsed, and reality has had a chance to chip away at the internet-haze of lust that you were caught in. You still want him. You still want the affair to be real. But now, you've remembered that you have a life. This time when he asks what you're wearing you shut him down, politely. Two days later he tries again. This time you fall into the old trap.

You say *we should text...messaging takes too long on Twitter. Do you still have my number?*

He says no. Crumple like a paper doll.

And then, try not to be hurt by this. It makes sense that he wouldn't keep your number. What if his wife looked in his phone one day? And what would he even file you under: your name, your twitter handle, as *that whore from the internet*? Give him your number; take another hit.

He asks for a photo of you naked, or at least stripped down to your red lace undies. Do not send one. Ignore his request. I don't have to tell you this. You are far less trusting than he is. You are smarter than he is. The rest will happen as it always does. In the moment, it will be a turn on. And when it's over, he will thank you. Do not be surprised. It will always end like this: painfully quick. Logically you know it makes sense, there is no such thing as sextuddling(?) (cuddlexting?) (spoonexting?). There is no cuddling after sexting. Regardless, you will still be bothered by his speedy retreat, his brush off. While your vagina is still wet, you will become all too aware of the things that this is not. This is not anything. And yet, it is not entirely nothing. Some days you wonder why you bother to return to this man and admonish yourself for your inability to disengage from his pull. He is a celebrity and if you are being honest, that is a big draw. But it is more than that. You've convinced yourself that he is a good person. You know that from his position of power he is fucking with you, even though he's not actually fucking you. But then he will be paying attention when you tweet about your sobriety or a life change and he will congratulate you. It will take him a mere second to send a message or tweet, but it feels like receiving a personal letter in the mail.

You will feel special. You will think you are the only one. You are not the only one. There is no fucking way you are the only one. You know this. You have to know this. Jesus Christ tell me that you know this!

A month later, when the sting of his last *thank you* for sexting has dissipated, you send him a message. Maybe this is an addiction. Maybe you are delusional. Maybe you have big dreams and, really, who says that one day he won't be the hand you need getting up. Capitalize on your awkward persona.

You: *Can't believe you haven't noticed my adorable new avi ;) JUST KIDDING PLEASE DON'T UNFOLLOW ME!*

Him: *So cute!*

You: *And that's why you're my favorite!*

Him: *Lol*

You: *Well maybe number 2...but it's not really fair because Sean Connery has an accent...can you do an accent?*

Him: *Not really.*

You: *Just kidding obviously you're number one...Sean Connery is fictional.*

Silence. He does not respond. Wait half an hour and then message again.

You: *Not a fan of my Connery jokes? I knew I should've stopped while I was ahead.*

Silence. For the next few hours, check his tweets every so often to see if he's ignoring you. Check to see if he stars any other tweets. He won't do either. Become a little less crazy-hurt and agitated and go about your business. If he wants to respond he will. After all, why would he just suddenly start ignoring you?

The next morning, he messages: *Sorry I fell asleep, long day!*

Don't bother responding. Enjoy this rare moment of power (though the fact that you care enough to manipulate yourself into a more powerful position technically negates said power). He fell asleep during your witty banter and that's on him. You don't need to be angry about this. There is no need to harbor feelings of resentment. You can just leave it as is. His will be the last message left un-responded to. Feel powerful for a few minutes. After those minutes are over, go back to living your life as normal. You are a strong woman (most of the time).

Before you know it, it is May and a string of events will change everything. A girl on the Internet will write an article about body image. She will post it online with a picture of her eating pizza in her underwear. People will rally around her. She's a gorgeous size 8 and though she's saying great things about how women should feel wonderful about their own bodies, you will have concerns. Size 8 is not fat. You will wonder how people would react if an actual fat person posted their body so flagrantly. You will immediately write an article that conveys this. You will post a picture of your size 24 body in a bathing suit, at a BBQ, eating a messy burger off a paper plate on your lap. The photo will not be cropped, shopped, or filtered. The photo will not be flattering in the traditional sense. Your heart will nearly stop beating. He will read your words and see your fat body for the first time, and then he will retweet the article to his now 70,000 followers. The response will be deafening. He will tweet an endorsement about how much he loves it, and then he will message you. He will tell you that he loves it. Several exclamation marks of love. Thank him. He will reiterate his love; you will reiterate your thanks.

Leave this as the final message. Do not pursue him further. Do not ruin the picture you have of him in your mind. Sure, you will probably send innocuous messages back and forth with him: a *Congratulations!* here and a *Happy Birthday* there. But, in the sweetness, let this be how it ends.

# LOVE POEMS FOR BUTCHERS

# FITNESS TIPS FOR MOUNTAIN LIONS

On a Monday in April, send your friend pictures of the hottest twenty-five-year-old you have ever seen. Ask permission to foster this lust. You are thirty-two years old and ill equipped for this. Ask as few questions as possible from people whose answers you do not like. When a girl in your writing workshop asks if you have earned this cliché, avert your eyes and manage your nerves with donuts. Be good (but not so good that it's off-putting).

Find a way to discuss your predilection for good teeth (but not in a weird way). Tell almost no one about the thing you're thinking of doing and do almost nothing but think about doing it. Dread it; want it; put it off. When it begins to feel like this is a thing you cannot do, remember that twenty-five is not nearly as young as it feels. Twenty-five-year-old men are adults—their brains have fully formed (that's just science). Move away from the novelty of it all. Never say cougar. There is value in this thing. Do not pull at your own loose threads. Keep a bottle of superglue on your nightstand. Forget nothing.

You are a cement statue, a spine made of steel, but your heart is an IKEA futon. There is danger in having so much fun immediately after finishing your master's degree. You will have spent months, years even, working towards this moment, and when it's over, the sigh of relief will be so huge that the exhale turns you inside out. Now is not the time to buy a motorcycle. Now is not the time to dabble in heroin. The joy of this will be too great and the lull that follows will wreck you. Still, you will do it.

Be prepared for him to be fun and relaxed. He is twenty-five and doesn't yet know what it is to be a disappointment to his parents. He is a twenty-five-year-old who has made really great life choices. His two bachelor's degrees match your two bachelor's degrees like a game of academic Connect Four; he is no regular baby boy.

He will make the first move by sending a message, having found you on a dating website only days after you posted a new profile. He will not objectify you but instead ask questions about your life: he will be kind; he will be sweet; he will be interesting. Eager but timid, he will tell you that he was unsure whether someone your age could be interested in him, *but* he will add, he couldn't help but try. And you will melt (just a little). You are too easily swayed by the bare minimum.

*When are you free?* He will ask, and you will lie to buy yourself time.

*Thursday and Friday night* is what you say though you are free all the nights until then. You will think that giving yourself three days is enough time to become an entirely different person, someone thinner and at least a little bit better. You have never been more reasonable.

Disappointed, he types: *I'm hanging out with my friends on Thursday night, and I'm leaving for Gatineau on Friday.*

You let the words just sit there. It would be kind of you to change your fake plans for him, but you are not so kind, and he is still yet a stranger. And so, you will not budge.

*Oh* and then a sad face emoticon is all you type.

He will type: *Let me see what I can do,* and you will go back to eating candy, and celebrating the fact that you have completed your master's degree. You won't need to worry about looking good for a twenty-five-year-old (if sagging breasts could sigh).

Except, he will change his plans. He will rearrange his friends like a living room. He will open up his Thursday night and your heart. He will make you forget that you are overweight and tired, that you are fragile and out-of-practice, that you are not ready to handle this kind of fun. He will make you a better person.

On your first date, in an Irish pub on Saint Laurent, when your smiles bounce back and forth off each other, he will lean in a little closer to the table and tell you again that tomorrow he is leaving for Gatineau. You will smile because you think he is returning home to visit, but you are wrong. He is leaving for the summer; he has finished his degree; he is leaving for good. He is removing his bed and his couch and the possibility of calling on a Wednesday night to invite you over for spaghetti and sex (or, sex and spaghetti). He is taking away the things you don't yet know you want. The possibilities are still endless, but the likelies have become unlikely.

"But," he says, "I come back to Montreal all the time," and you are both made light by hope.

Try not to fall in love with the person that he sees on the first date. Do not move in for a closer look at your reflection in his pretty blue eyes. When you tell him about your plans for adventure, how you're going to move up North and then eventually traverse the globe, his face will light up and his eyes will sparkle. Do not lean into it. His support is a false positive. He is not invested in your survival. He has no idea if you can actually do this. He will look at you like you have never had a horrible idea, never thought about stretching yourself too thin or reaching too far, never fucked anything up. Do not warm yourself in his glow.

Try not to fidget so much. When he leaves the table to go to the bathroom, readjust yourself. Pull at your bra straps and try to make your boobs look perkier, younger, better. And then when you cannot (because that's insane), just relax in knowing that these are the same boobs you had when he asked you out. Stop doubting yourself so much. When the strap on your brand-new dress breaks, do not panic. Ask the waitress if she has a safety pin, and when she replies no and walks away, do not give up. Ask for a stapler. Tell her that this is a first date and that it is going amazingly well. Emphasize "*AMAZINGLY!*" so she knows, I mean really knows, that you're on one of those dates. Make sure she understands that this date is worth something. This date has real value, and it requires a team effort. She will nod and bring you a stapler from behind the bar. She will help you put your dress back together. This is open-heart surgery. When he returns to the table, he will have no idea that the right side of your dress is being held up by a can-do attitude.

Let his desire for fun make you buoyant. He will say, "On the off chance," and then point to his pocket, "that you wanted to, I brought a joint." He will want to go back to your apartment to smoke and say something about his roommate having a date over. "Otherwise, we could just go to my place," he'll say.

You must not let him come over. You must explain away the possibility of going back to your apartment. Say something about how you're not comfortable bringing a relative stranger home on the first date. Say something about how you didn't have time to clean. Talk about how you like to go slow, how you don't fuck on the first date, about some blah blah bullshit that is only the tiniest sliver of the real reasons: you have your period, you don't yet know if he's ever seen a fat girl naked, your apartment is too small for a person your age, you aren't ready for him to know anything less than the best part of you. Offer everything but the truth. Try not to call yourself a lady because you are no lady (not to mention your feminist guilt over saying it like that, like ladies don't like orgasms or something). Never mention your heart. Do not confide that you were thinking you might want to date him, and you haven't yet wrapped your head around the whole moving-to-Gatineau bomb. Do not mention how attracted to him you are. Do not reveal that you may already like him too much. Smile, shrug your shoulders, and look open but without any good ideas. Do your best to appear youthful.

"That's okay," he will say, smiling down at you, his blond hair practically a halo. "We can go to a park around here." He doesn't wink but it will feel like it.

When the waitress comes, he will ask for the bill in French. You have lived in Montreal for almost two years and French has never sounded so sexy. You have heard people mock French Canadian accents and never understood the impulse. Wonder if this is what it is to love a fat girl, to see fireworks where others only see wobbly lines. You will wish you could record his voice. Long before you are at the end, you will start to think of souvenirs and pieces of him that you could keep. He will pay for the bill with a fifty, which you assume could only have been a gift from his grandmother, and then ask again if you want to go for a walk. He will stand to create space for you. He will wait while you put on your jacket.

Outside in the street, he will stand close and say, "I think there's one just around the corner." Do not waste time worrying that his long steps will outpace your chubby strides, or that you should be sucking in your round belly and instead give in to this fun. Let out your breath. Let down your shoulders. Stop counting the clock.

When the two of you walk up the cobblestone street, and he points out a college bar he not-too-long-ago frequented, do not mention that the people standing outside look like teenagers. Do not draw his attention to the fact that you are rapidly aging before his very eyes.

North of Sherbrooke, at the end of the cobblestone

street between Avenue Laval and St. Denis, there is a park with a fountain called Square Saint Louis. In April, when it is technically spring, the fountain will be dry and full of leaves and hope (but mostly just leaves). He will nuzzle your cheek and note with surprise how soft your skin is, as if he had expected a thirty-two-year-old to be made of sandpaper and wisdom.

When he says that you're a good kisser, do not mention how many extra years you've had to practice. Turn to him, sitting on a cold park bench and forget everything except how good it feels pressing your body against his. When he giggles, let it shake you.

"We can watch a movie?" he will say innocently, eyebrows raised and not really asking.

"You can come over next time," the words dribbling out your mouth between kisses.

"Movie night," he will say—that smile of his, a goddamn spotlight.

Kiss him for hours that feel like minutes, till the cold seeps in, and he shivers against you. Lick the salt on your lips from his runny nose as he burrows himself around your warm flesh, your squishy bits, the parts of you that need only a sweatshirt when his thinness needs a winter coat. Run your fingers through his downy hair. Briefly wonder if his mother looks like you.

Long after it has gotten cold, and you get up from the park bench, he will ask you, "Which bus do you take?" and then, "I'll walk you."

He will stand tall behind you reaching his arms under yours, his hands around your belly like a resting place. His palms will press flat against your slowing metabolism, his fingers stretching across your marks. He will kiss your neck and move his legs behind yours, the two of you walking like toy soldiers or people in love. This is a first date with a twenty-five-year-old. Try not to die before it's over.

If you walk to the northwest corner of Sherbrooke and St. Denis, there is a bus stop where the two of you will make people uncomfortable, making out like teenagers, which is coincidentally the double of the difference in your ages. Twenty-five has never looked so good to you. With his back against the pole and your chest pressed against his, you will feel like you're seventeen again. He will seem older, his head half a foot above yours. When he looks down at your face, avert your eyes. His gaze, too good. Your reflection, a funhouse mirror.

When the bus comes and his lips linger on yours, you will have to be the one to pull away. Laugh and say, "I have to get on the bus…the bus is here…I have to get on the bus."

He will continue to steal kisses. He will grab at your hand. Do not let your heart fall out onto the pavement. Button up—everyone can see inside you.

When you arrive home, he will text to find out about your safe arrival, and you will think him mature. You will think him smitten with you. Do not make assumptions based on words. You are a writer and should know better. Do not read into his exclamation points. I shouldn't have to tell you this. You are too old not to already know this.

The next day will be uncertain. He said he would come back to Montreal. He said he would come back, but you can't remember if he had added, "For you." You can't remember if he is returning for the city or your embrace. You let him get you high and now you can think of nothing else. All day you will tell yourself not to text, not to reach out. But you can't get the taste off your tongue. He is in your veins. And so, you will give in.

When he responds, he will seem older and further away—the language barrier now decidedly more pronounced. When you ask about his return to Montreal, you will be disappointed by his uncertain response. Do not to blow it out of proportion. Bear in mind the lack of tone and the fact that he is two and a half hours away. You will ask what is holding up the decision; you will want to know why he isn't moving mountains to be with you. He will respond something about work: scheduling, co-workers, and legitimate things. Rub some dirt on your feelings; you are fine.

And then, just like that, he is coming back to Montreal.

He types: *Monday night?*

You type: *Sounds great.*

And on Monday night he will come.

He will knock on your door and hand you a bottle of Coke Zero and two packages of microwave popcorn like they're a bouquet of roses. You are far too swayable a judge. Do not give perfect tens so easily. Find a way to expect more from people. His thoughtfulness is a trap. Tell your excitement to put its clothes back on.

When he steps into your apartment, make your arms wide and gesture at length to hide your embarrassment over its size. Keep your weird jokes to yourself. Do not say that your apartment is like a penis (in so much as everyone wishes it was bigger). Show him the balcony, point out the view, show him his city from the place where you have watched it for the last two years. On the fourteenth floor, looking south towards the Saint Lawrence, stand so close to him that you can feel the static between your arm hair and then wait for his reach. Do not let your muscles fall lax. This is the moment of the one-two punch, a direct hit to the gut, that place where you should have abs but instead have sandwiches. This attraction is a minefield. You cannot take this swooning to the bank.

He is sweet to bring the popcorn, but you do not own a microwave. You will have to pop the popcorn the old-fashioned way. He will ask if you have butter, and you will stumble with your answer.

"I have something *like* butter," you will say reaching into your small fridge, in your tiny apartment with your doll-sized IKEA furniture, and pull out a container of Earth Balance, a vegan non-dairy spread. You are not a vegan, but sometimes you dabble. When he asks how to melt it, point to the one-egg-sized frying pan that only covers one-quarter of an element as it heats. When he asks for salt, show him your 'no-salt salt alternative.' You will look around your apartment and be painfully aware that everything in it feels just a little bit less than. College-kid furniture, walls decorated like the locker of a teenage girl, nothing quite good enough. He was probably expecting riches, and wisdom, and the kind of life you expect men seven years your senior to have. You have none of these things. You have degrees. You have several degrees and an unmanageable student loan. You are too old to have so little. Feel old, nearly ancient, practically on the edge of death, and ashamed;

feel like a fraud. And then let it go (because what else is there but to let it go?).

The two of you smoke on the balcony and then go back into your apartment. There's barely a moment to take a breath before he's kissing you again, his tongue filling up all your insecure places. When you run your fingers over his abs, he will smile and say something about how he broke his foot and hasn't been playing soccer. He will make note of his inadequacies. Something about "...fifteen pounds heavier when I'm working out..." he will say, unrolling his vulnerabilities before you like a sleeping bag. Whitewash away his insecurities as he has done for you.

Standing in the middle of your apartment, he will push your sweater from your shoulders. When he tries to undo your jeans and struggles with the button until you have to point out that the waistband has been rolled over, do not choke on your embarrassment. Say something like "I've lost some weight recently," and while this is true it's not entirely the reason. The truth is a lifetime of plus size clothes, things never fitting quite right, the cut, the fabric, a lifetime of rolling things over at the waist so that they fit right in the crotch. But do not say this. Say something about weight loss. Say something that sounds better than I'm fat and the world doesn't understand me. Say something quickly and undo the jeans yourself. You're fine. Do not tap at your raw places.

Lose your pants and inhibitions in one dance step. Kiss until kissing seems like a thing you two invented but do not get swept away. You are not wearing a lifejacket. Take off your rose-colored glasses but ignore every hiccup in this love affair. He is young and imperfect; he will make missteps. He will have typical moments. He will be an everyman. Somewhere after the third time you've blown him, he will suggest that you must watch a lot of porn. Take this as a compliment. He will mean that he has enjoyed himself. Maneuver past every mistake.

When he reaches down to return the favor, you will have to utter some of the most painful words you have ever had to say. You will have to tell this beauty of a twenty-five-year-old that you are a woman, bleeding.

Say: My womb is ripping me apart

Say: My womb is ripping

Say: We must remain apart

You will have to say that you cannot, should not, will not.

"At least, not tonight," you will say.

When he is disappointed, relish in having been wanted. When you had agreed to him coming over tonight, you were playing Russian roulette with your period, and you lost. But it was hardly your fault. You are an addict after one hit, and now you have to say the things you never wanted to say. Do not reveal that you are a woman, that you have a body, that you are a human being. Assume twenty-five-year-old men cannot handle the truth. And maybe you will be right to do so. Maybe he's only ever been with young, thin girls with taut, perky breasts whose skinny bodies don't bleed so regularly, and time has not touched their skin—no mark, no stretch, no scar, no sag.

He will run his hand up your leg, move from your knee to your thigh, and note how warm you are. The heat and the sweat, which you hate, is a comfort to him. He will lie back, fold you into his chest, and wrap you up with one arm. Breathe in every pheromone. Everything will be perfect, until the breathing and movements get too heavy, until it seems like he has forgotten that you are a woman, bleeding. His hands will again wander too close for comfort. You will worry that he'll leave this night with blood on his hands. You don't want his memories of you to look like a murder scene.

It will be difficult to concentrate on your own body when his is always so close nearby. Watch him out of the corner of your eye as he eats popcorn with a kind of shirtless glee. Do not lick the salt off his fingers. Do not entirely forget your butter belly. This joy will drain like a pool at the end of summer. Do not belly flop into this fun. Find a place to hang on.

It'll happen when he's rolling a joint and you're standing in your panties, breasts sagging for all to see. While he works diligently, think about the last few weeks, about how much you will miss Montreal. Say this out loud. Say that you'll miss your friends, the city, this kind of fun. Say it casually. Mean nothing by it. You are impulsive in this happiness.

"But, you're thirty-two and I'm twenty-five, so this can never be more than just fun."

He drops it like a bomb. This is a warzone, and you are only wearing underwear. Second-guess everything. Had you asked him for some kind of commitment? Had you made any suggestion that you were looking for something more than fun? Had you ripped open your chest and thrown your heart at his feet, throbbing and desperate? Laugh awkwardly and get a glass of water from the kitchen. Try to quiet the ringing in your ears. Assess the damage at the scene. Pretend he didn't use your age against you as if it was a thing that makes you entirely unlovable. Pretend your age isn't a weapon. Do not drop to the floor—no shots have been fired.

Let it go. Try to let it go. Do your best to let it go. And then, when you cannot let it go, try not to make a big deal about it.

Say: I'm still leaving Montreal

Say: I'm still leaving

Say: Au revoir

You will say, "I didn't mean anything by that."

He will say, "I know."

Just like that, casual, with a look on his face saying of course not. His eyes will say obviously, but your ears will not forget. Your heart, a little nicked; your ego, a peach. Stand there shell-shocked, a pitchfork through both of your feet. Only, what else is there but to let it go? Develop amnesia and wrap yourself in clearance rack, polka dot sheets. Press your breasts into his ribs, lay one arm across his chest, propped up, his bones a real support.

He will say, "This is so sexy, you are so sexy," and his accent will vibrate across your cheeks. Remember the way his voice sounds.

He is wearing shorts now, had put them on when you paused the movie to smoke again. He will say something about how comfortable he finds them. Weird and innocent, he will say something about how much he likes wearing shorts as if it makes him unique, as if the experience is entirely his own: the innocence of a declaration of pleasure, the inexperience of boys' basketball shorts.

The kisses will go on all night and you will enjoy them all night because kissing is all there is. Your period becomes a blessing because this will be one of the only nights you spend with a man where you don't have to be the pace car. You don't have to be the one saying slow down, go slower, not yet. You can relax. You can relax. You can finally fucking relax (as long as your tampon holds).

Somewhere before the morning, in your too small bed, in your too hot apartment, this twenty-five-year-old will kiss you goodnight and then purposely fall asleep in your bed. Act his age and leave your makeup on. Sleep with your contacts in. Try not to die in your sleep.

The next morning, after he leaves, you will spend the day feeling like magic. But, when he doesn't text in reassurance of how amazing you are, you will feel less so. I warned you not to do this. I warned you not to have this kind of fun so soon after finishing your master's degree. I warned you about the intensity this lust would create. Do not say I didn't warn you.

Time will cease to exist, inasmuch as it has become infinite and never seems to move an inch. You will have gone from devoting all your time to your job and your studies, to having nothing to do but think about trying to become a writer and how obviously every decision you've ever made to bring you to this point was worthless (what the fuck does one do with a Master of Arts in English Literature anyway?) Do not watch the clock. Those hands will not hold yours.

He will text again. When he does, the messages will be polite and friendly. No, they will be more than that. He asks questions, he pays attention. But still, you can't help but feel as if you are bothering him. You are a thirty-two-year-old hassle. Has anything ever been more pathetic? Or perhaps you are being too sensitive. Perhaps it is the situation (given that he lives two and a half hours away and has a full-time job), or perhaps it is the language barrier (his exclamation points as misplaced as your lust). Reel yourself in. Do not give in to this lull. The joy was too great, and now you are struggling not to lose your shit in public. At night you tap your veins hoping to shake something loose. Logic will tell you that it is school, or the complete lack of it, that leaves you with this empty uncertain feeling in your chest. Your future is unclear; you are adrift. But your feet will find the ground again. You will sober up.

First though, you will be ripped inside out. You met a man you barely know, whose presence you only barely experienced, and still your whole body will ache from his lack. You will search day and night to find a way to justify the horrible pain his absence has left (though logically you know it has little to do with him). The texting will peter out causing you to feel even more ecstatic every time he does make contact. Find joy anywhere you can. When you receive his text after a long lull, while sitting in a pub with your friends, and your hands shoot up into the air uncontrollably as if your team had scored a touchdown, laugh until it hurts. Let the laughter re-inflate you. It's okay to find humor in the pain.

Don't look for the reasons he hasn't fallen in love with you: your laugh, too loud; your tongue, too sloppy; you can't keep a secret. Don't take everything so personal (when he made that crack about your age as if being thirty-two precluded you from being of value, he didn't mean it and even if he did, he was wrong). Tell me you know that he was wrong.

Learn to deal with this disappointment. Wail like an indulgent toddler (when no one is looking). Sob from your soft spots and let everything loose. I told you not to do this, but you did this, and now all you can do is wait for it to be over. This feeling isn't all from him. In fact, most of it will have nothing to do with him. This is your resetting point. You accomplished a dream and in doing so became untethered. You cannot speed up this process. He was the tipping point, and you fell face first into the cement sidewalk. Do not forget how he got you high. Let this push you forward. Let this be how you remember Montreal.

# LOVE POEMS FOR BUTCHERS

# HOW TO GIVE A PASSIVE AGGRESSIVE HANDJOB

Every profile picture seemed to be of a man wearing skinny jeans, and a beard he'd learned to grow from men's magazines. I just wanted someone to like my love poems about dish washing and residential taxes and the cost of airfare in the summer. I was uncomfortably fat, which only bothered me to the extent that it affected my breathing and my stature and my desire to spontaneously have sex with men who were never worthy. The kind of men who thought they were being lovely in the way they described a woman's full lips, her shape, her youth, like those were things she'd earned. I just wanted them to stop talking about tits and curves like they were peace prizes, like they could save us all. How was I supposed to relate to the kind of men who said, "I'm tall enough, so you can wear heels," as if that was a thing I worried about. Their lack of empathy for my bones was terrifying. I didn't want to go out with men who were busy telling women how to dress. They always seemed to talk a lot about things but never people, their words an ill-fitting suit, always just a little too tight in the crotch. I bet their heroes were drinking brown liquor in mahogany drawing rooms and pretending to have read books written by old white men. Everyone was always terribly miserable. We never wanted the same things.

I was looking for a five-cent-word-type-love, a temporary fix. I just wanted a little something for the pain, a salve to spread across my body to heal the disappointment. The twenty-five-year-old I had dated immediately after finishing my master's degree had wrecked me. As it turns out, the joy could not sustain the lull. And talking about it only ever made me feel more alone. Dating, they say (they, being me), is like someone putting a cheesecake on the table in front of you, and just when you're about to take a bite, a hand comes from out of nowhere and knocks it onto the ground. I wasn't upset that the cheesecake didn't love me, I was crushed that it was on the floor (probably covered in hair—because let's be honest, this metaphor doesn't make sense unless there's something more gross than just the cake being on the floor. I mean, I'd eat floor cake. I've eaten floor cake. But I couldn't eat this cake anymore. It wasn't even just floor cake. The cake was gone).

Message from *Dan* reads: *nice tits*

Message from *Richard* reads: *I love your curves*

Message from *Francois* reads: *mmm mmm yummy*

(I couldn't help but wonder if he thought I was a donut).

I message: *There's no way your parents aren't ashamed of*

*you.*

I message: *Just wait until you see my flats!*

I message: *Snooze.*

He messages: *I was just joking.*

But he doesn't know what humor is. He has said something stupid and thinks his laissez-faire attitude makes it a joke. He is all intention and no action, thinks wanting something to be true makes it so. The messages continue to come in from men who are never going to be a good match because they don't understand that kidding without being funny is just lying, and I am tired of lying with men who aren't funny. At best, I hoped to find someone who could make me laugh in a way that changed the very make up of my DNA. At worst, maybe there would be an adventure, someone I could tolerate long enough to stab late at night and leave bleeding on the page, the only way to make his story worth reading; a gesture of love. One man messaged to say that his *being interesting* should make up for him not being funny, which was a fair enough point. Except that after reading his profile, I was forced to remind him that a man who had written, *the prettier the girl, the more interesting the conversation* wasn't in any position to judge. I wanted better than him. I wanted my last few months in Montreal to be worth the rent.

The key to a passive aggressive handjob is the tension. You may have been thinking it was grip strength or rhythm, but you would be wrong. It's about balancing the present against the future. It's about how much you hate going on first dates, and if you can just find a way to not hate this man while he's lying there completely naked with his dick in your hand, and you're still completely dressed because this is a goddamn first date, then maybe, just maybe, you can go on a second date with him instead of a first date with someone else, someone new.

But I am no gymnast and there isn't a beam wide enough for all this rage and regret. He doesn't deserve my good palms, my silky spit, the silhouette of my body in his eye line. When it ends, he will cum into my hand, and I will let it spill onto his stomach. I will go to the bathroom and wash his jizz from my fingers. I won't offer him a towel. I don't know where he keeps them. This is a first date; I don't even know his last name.

The night we met at a bar, near the Jean-Talon market, he was dressed like a man. He was dressed like a man in pants and a shirt. I think it was a polo shirt but it's kind of hard to remember. It's kind of hard to remember because it wasn't anything special; he wasn't anything special. He wasn't awful, well he kind of was, but for later and different reasons. He wasn't dressed awful; I just don't remember. I want to say maroon. I want to say a maroon shirt and beige pants, but can that even be true? I can't remember. He wasn't worth remembering. That seems harsh. I don't want to be cruel. It's funny how much I worry about being cruel, how much I worry about treating them decently. I write love poems for butchers and everyone worries about their cut fingers and dirty aprons. They don't worry about me. They cut into me like a fatty steak. They set me on fire. If you're quiet, you can hear the sizzle.

The truth is that I was desperate (refrain). It seemed like I was always feeling desperate when it came to finding happiness and dating but this time the desperation was specific; it was time sensitive. I had been feeling like shit for weeks, or was it only a few days? Time becomes taffy after heartbreak. I would've done almost anything to be out of the lull that followed in the wake of the last man I had dated.

When I saved Henri as a favorite on Plenty of Fish, I hadn't thought much of it. He was attractive with a witty enough profile, which is to say that I liked his jaw line and a joke he had made about football (soccer). When he messaged almost immediately, it felt like he couldn't control his excitement.

At the bar, we talked about our commonalities. I was thinking about moving up North, for the isolation money and the adventure of it, and he had already been there, was able to offer perspective and foreshadowing. I thought he had gone up North to work as a scientist, given that he'd just finished his MSc in Microbiology, but as it turned out he had moved up there for a girl. He was from Spain and chided me for not picking up much French in my two years in Montreal. I didn't make the joke about how I was trying to pick up as many of them as I could. I didn't think he'd laugh. I wasn't sure anyone would laugh. Lately, I'd been much less funny. He spoke three languages and was working on a fourth. When the bar got loud and a band started to play, we left.

He said, "Want to come back to my place?" before we had walked more than a few steps, and then gestured up the street. "I live right over there." I was shocked to find out he lived so close to the bar he asked me to meet him in and tried not to resent him for making me trek the furthest north I'd ever been in Montreal for our date. A nice guy would've met me halfway. A nice guy wouldn't have made me come so far. Men are so quick to think themselves nice. The entitlement is always what gets me. Kindness is a basic human quality, a reason you're not a terrible person, not a reason someone should want to date you. The bar seemed to be set so low; I worried about bruising my shins. While we walked, I thought about which bus I would take back south so that I could stop at that bagel place on Fairmount that's open all night and makes those chocolate chip bagels with a hint of orange.

Inside his apartment, I walked the length of the living room and then back again, trying to keep his dog, who was pawing at me, from snagging my dress. I stood there, waiting awkwardly, while he poured himself a beer and then me a glass of water, not sure if I should take a seat on the couch yet.

"I really like to cook," he said gesturing at something on a cutting board but never offering me anything to eat.

"Oh yeah?" I was trying to sound like one of those people who are interested in cooking. He put his dog in a cage in the bedroom, which seemed kind of cruel, though beneficial for my lace dress, which he (the dog) may have already snagged. I didn't look down. I didn't want to be sad on a first date.

At the bar, I hadn't been so sure that he liked me. There was a stiffness in his body, a lack of an endearing sweetness. He seemed to be all corners, awkward but self-assured. But back at his apartment, sitting on his white leather couch, he was all cushion. In his apartment, with the lights too bright, he seemed smaller; his limbs, thinner; he seemed just a little bit shorter. But then he smiled and the difference from the bar to home hardly seemed to matter. As soon as the movie started, I could feel him thinking about how to kiss me.

An hour went by while I could feel him thinking and plotting and devising. I never turned to look at him. I wanted him to kiss me but not immediately. I was orchestrating tension, which is less psychotic and more burdensome than it sounds. If it were up to him, it would happen right away. I wanted it to happen (maybe, probably, don't rush me). I could feel his desire in every movement: a hand near my thigh, and then on my thigh, the subtle shift in his body while he considered putting an arm behind my head and then the shift again when he reconsidered and did nothing, the slow loss of inches between us as he moved closer on the couch, and then his hand on mine, and finally our fingers together, laced.

An hour later, I looked at him, and he kissed me. It was a little too rough, a little too aggressive. Everything felt sloppy, like I was being jostled. I tried to recall how many beers he had had at the bar (maybe two?). That wasn't enough to explain the way his lips never quite fit with mine, the repeated bumping of our teeth, the way his tongue slipped around like a fish—first heavily on top of mine, then flapping about in the corners of my mouth, then as if it was lining my lips. His hands moved down the length of my dress until they found an opening. We had barely begun kissing and he wanted legs and thighs, the whole chicken dinner. I said the first thing I could think of.

"I haven't shaved my legs."

"I don't care," he said.

Because of course he didn't. Because of course they never do, but, after all, that isn't really the point. It's not about whether or not he cares that I've shaved my legs, but that I don't want him touching my unshaven legs (or, that I have to make up some bullshit, or purposely not shave my legs, in order to keep him from going beyond my limits when my words don't suffice). My words did little to change the pace. I pushed his hands away and then pulled back on the kissing to show I was serious, and this time he stopped pushing further. I liked him less for not immediately heeding my words and myself less for not leaving.

After a while the kissing started to improve, our rhythms becoming just a little more in sync. Just when I had begun to enjoy the making out, he pulled his lips from mine and asked, "Bedroom?" He slid to the edge of the couch and stood, pulling at me a little. I chided myself for not being better than this, for not thinking faster than this, for not leaving sooner than this. In the bedroom, I saw his dog in the cage.

The dog whined. I felt bad. He continued to kiss me unfazed.

The first step in giving a passive aggressive handjob is to want him (maybe, possibly, in theory). When I tell this story later, to friends, they act horrified. "How awful!" they exclaim. "You should've just left." Which is both true and not so simple. Because it's not like I didn't want him to touch my legs ever, or that I wouldn't (maybe) want to have sex with him at some point (maybe) I just didn't want it to happen tonight, on the first date.

Other friends suggest that I just shouldn't go back to someone's apartment on the first date. But why is agreeing to watch a movie and even make out, an admission ticket for sex? Why should I not expect more from men, to think that I can be alone with them and not instantly (or ever) be expected to fuck? And before you say, "But then you can't fault men for—" stop that nonsense right now. Men are human beings with thoughts and feelings and decision-making abilities. Every day I manage to refrain from acting on any number of urges (mostly to murder people), and I think the least I should be able to expect from a man (yes, the absolute bare-fucking-minimum!), is to not have to repeat myself when I say, "No." I don't owe anyone any kind of explanation for why I might not want to fuck immediately after saying hello (no matter how many times I offer one anyway). I don't owe men shit. Fist in the air.

The second step of a passive aggressive handjob is to demonstrate your apathy. We were on the bed kissing, and then the next second he was standing up taking off all his clothes, and then before I could utter a word, he was back on the bed with me, buck naked. It was like a magic trick; now you see these clothes, now you don't. One minute this was a normal first date, and the next he was completely naked while I remained fully dressed, not even a nipple out of place. Nothing says apathy quite like remaining clothed while the man you're kissing is completely naked. No fucks given.

The third step is to give absolutely no more than a decent effort. This step is the trickiest because if you're not great at giving handjobs, by not giving it your full effort you could end up extending the whole affair and that benefits no one, least of all you. If, like me, you've managed to be pretty good at this act of 'driving him standard' then go ahead and give a little less-than. You want him to cum quickly because this is terrible, but you don't want it to be so good as to give him a great deal of pleasure because—let's be honest—he doesn't even deserve the half-assed handjob you're giving him to begin with. In fact, get up. My god just get up and leave! Fuck this stupid advice. Be a better person than me! Be stronger. Have more forethought. Get out of there and stop breaking yourself against the bodies of men who do not deserve your conversation, your wit, your charm, your expertly skilled palms. Get out now, I beg of you. Please. *Please.*

But if you can't, if you're like me and find yourself in this scenario over and over again for any number of reasons—forgive yourself. Do it immediately. Let yourself off the hook. Just like that. You're okay. You're great. I love you. Look in the mirror. I love you. Know that I love you. *I love you.*

That night in Henri's bedroom, after he cums and I wash my hands, he gets dressed. I was already dressed. I was still dressed. I never became dress-less. While I held his dick in my hand and we kissed and he moaned, I never lost a single article. He tried to go up my dress (but I hadn't shaved my legs and I was wearing spandex shorts pulled up to my bra, and let's not forget the all-important—I DIDN'T FUCKING WANT HIM TO). He tried to get at my bra, but what was the point, if I didn't want to take off my dress, I obviously didn't want him inside my bra. And so, I took off nothing, because, after all, that was exactly how much I had wanted to take off.

We returned to the couch and started watching the movie somewhere close to where we had left off. Within minutes, his head was bobbing forward and then lurching back again like a sea captain asleep at the wheel. I was hurt, at first, taking his drowsiness as a personal slight, he obviously didn't like me or my passive-aggressive handjob. Then, I was irritated because I had wanted to see how the movie ended. Eventually though, I was saddened that this guy was my dating demographic, and I was starting to wonder about the genius of women who date young men. Young men don't fall asleep after cumming. Young men stay awake for as long as you need. Young men are the future.

But I'm not completely heartless, I knew that he had had this wonderful release and probably would've given almost anything to be able to go to sleep. And because by some miracle of miracles I actually didn't hate him yet (how was that even possible?!?). And because I had managed, in the most fucked up of ways, to view his inability to read my body language and aggressive sexual advances on me as signs of uncontrollable attraction (rather than see them for what they really are, which is selfishness and an aggressive lack of empathy, not to mention obvious undervaluing of me as a person)—I said, "I'm going to let you get some sleep," and then patted his knee. I was thinking myself adorable. I was feeling entirely dominant after the passive-aggressive handjob. He shattered the delusion within moments.

Honestly, I had expected him to walk me to the bus stop. Not always, not after every date, but because I didn't know the area, and because I'd come out all this way, and because he'd just cum all over himself thanks to me. Instead, I got a few quick directions and barely enough time to lace up my sandals. Apparently, he had a few passive-aggressive moves of his own. We kissed each other goodnight (or, maybe I kissed him, and he complied?). Suddenly, everything felt a little off; the power dynamics had definitely shifted.

I walked to the bus stop with my head held high. I

certainly wasn't going to feel bad if a guy didn't like me because I had given him a handjob I hadn't wanted to give in the first place. Everything is fine, I thought, walking the two blocks to my stop. This still counts as a good first date, nothing to feel upset over. Maybe he was just tired. Maybe he was just too relaxed. Maybe he was just a real fucking asshole. Tough to say. I walked two more blocks, thinking it a little weird that I hadn't yet run into the street he told me to catch my bus on. I thought about the bagels. After four more blocks, I started to sweat, wearing a denim jacket for the sole reason that it looked cute, and not at all because I was cold. My feet hurt—these were dating sandals not walking sandals.

I continued to walk around for another twenty minutes trying to spot anything familiar or at least a bus-stop with any kind of numbered route that I recognized. On the brink of angry tears, I caved and took a cab. When the driver asked, "Where to?" I said Sherbrooke, to which he asked, "Where to on Sherbrooke?"

"The closest point to us!" I was practically yelling. As

a poor grad student, a taxi ride wasn't how I wanted to spend what few dollars I had. I figured if I could just get him to take me to a street I knew, I could take a bus from there and the damage wouldn't be too bad. Ten minutes later he was dropping me off and while I would've rather spent that $10 on bagels, it wasn't the worst money I'd ever spent.

Already somewhat hysterical, I got out of the taxi, and was immediately accosted by a man who gasped in delight and exclaimed, "You look like a princess!" And perhaps he was just making an accurate assessment. Dressed in a white lace summer dress, which had mostly managed to avoid peril at the paws of a dog, I probably did look a bit like a princess. But I didn't have any more room for this man. I didn't have any space left for men to take up because they hadn't thought about how their words and presence were a burden. They had already taken too much. Every date started off so great, with such high hopes that I might meet a man who could treat me decently, who wasn't always a hundred percent out for his own interests, who had even the tiniest bit of empathy for my experience. I didn't have any more room to give; I was too full of disappointment. I made a noise of disgust and devastation, a guffaw and sigh so loud it almost hurt, crossed the street, and hoped he wouldn't follow me.

I never saw Henri again, though he remains on my Facebook. Perhaps he has clicked *unfollow* a while ago and thus forgotten that we are even friends. Perhaps he just wants to see how it all turns out for me. I could guess forever and still probably never hit the mark. People are, as they have always been, a goddamn mystery to me.

# FUCKING LIKE A WORKOUT PLAN

The first time we message is in March. He is the pursuer.

He says, *let's go out.*

He says, *I want to meet you.*

*Why should I want to?* I demand it like a petulant child.

He says, *I'm funny and smart and we'll have a good time.*

But they all say that. And I've never met a man who didn't think he was funny. Women spend our entire lives trying to live up to the expectations of the world—quiet your voice, make your arms into twigs, only when you're a ghost will you be loveable. Men are born to feel like presidents—dicks like hammers, jokes like fireworks. He doesn't ask enough questions. He is too quick to meet. He says things like, *and my dick game is strong*, but I don't find his arrogance endearing.

Only a week or two out of my thesis defense, I am still heavy into the grind of grad school. I have my own workshops to attend and classes to teach. There are, what feels like, a million papers to grade, spread out in seemingly manageable piles on my bed. I have a waistline that only believes in winter. Nothing in my closet fits right. I message *no thanks* and turn him down quickly.

The next time we message is in May when I have graduated and I'm an entirely new person. I am not working, but instead having fun in Montreal before I move back to Vancouver; there is joy in my every breath. I tell him as much. I message and say that I am a good person now, in case he wants to give me a second chance.

I say, *we should do this*, and he responds with banter. Maybe he is smart and funny after all? My hope is too quick and too close.

I give him my phone number and say *text me instead*. When instead of texting he keeps responding online, I figure that while it was possible that he had a girlfriend (or, theoretically worse, a wife), it was more likely that he had treated women poorly in the past, and they had gotten (understandably) upset and hysterical. Thus, he was hesitant to give out his phone number (because he was a real asshole). But for all my intents and purposes, this wasn't a problem. I was leaving. I was leaving. After all, I was leaving.

Still, his sweet smile and dimpled cheeks made me nervous. Without a phone number to make him a person, he wasn't entirely real—he wasn't tethered to anything. I didn't like people who couldn't be found out—when had they ever not had something to hide?

When I was twenty, I accidentally dated a man who

was married. When that man messaged me a few years ago on Facebook, he asked if I remembered him though he was certain I didn't. But a girl hardly forgets the first man to fake being sent off to the war in Iraq to hide his marriage. A girl hardly forgets the way she's been bruised by men. A girl hardly forgets anything.

At dinner, he leans forward on the table, taking up space like a man who's never been told to step aside. He smiles at all the right times and is enthusiastic about everything I say. He looks like a supermodel or a soccer star, his dark eyelashes longer than mine. I feel like the universe, in which I put no stock, and karma, in which I don't believe, have coupled together to bring me happiness. Finally, I sigh. Finally. And then I spill salsa on my dress.

"So, what are you into?" he asks.

"Pirates," I say, and he laughs because it's funny.

In the car ride home, he asks, too early, about all the things you want to know about a person you might end up fucking. He taints the date too soon, turns it from magic to typical with a few questions. He wants to know what kind of guys I'm attracted to (him, among others).

He wants to know if I've ever had a threesome (yes) and did I ever want to again (no). I tell him that threesomes are too performative, and that I don't like to share the spotlight, not to mention the more obvious problem of not actually being attracted to women (no matter how much I jokingly, and, worry, offensively, wish I could be). He says some things I want to hear (that he's into big girls, like really into them), and some things I could live without ever knowing (he tells me that he had a threesome once and though he, "did his duty," with both girls, he wasn't really attracted to the thinner one). He probably wants me to feel superior and secure, but instead I just feel bad for the thin girl—how he hadn't really wanted her, about all the fucking that was never as good as it should be, about how we let these things happen to us. It made me think of all the times I was someone's fat thin-girl.

We step into my apartment and in the seconds before he follows behind me, my eyes dart around and lock on the most embarrassing of sights: the Kleenex that didn't quite hit the bin, the dishes in the sink, the vibrator on the nightstand (the nightstand that is just two cardboard boxes stacked together).

"Don't be nervous," he says coming up behind me.

"I'm not," I lie because he wouldn't understand any of the reasons that I am. He'll think I'm nervous because this is all so new and daring and isn't he just so limitless and open-minded—a real sexual dynamo—when in actuality, I'm nervous that my shitty IKEA bed might break, or that he won't be as nice as he has been all night, or that when it's over I'll be filled with regret for any number of reasons. I'm worried he won't understand female anatomy and won't be receptive to my desires, or perhaps even worse, that I won't find a voice to speak up if things are not feeling great or if I start to feel pressured because I'm taking too long to cum or he wants to do something I don't like. So, I lie. When he tells me not to be nervous but says it like a question, I lie and say that I'm not, and then he leads me over to my own bed, and I have to pick up my dress like Cinderella on the steps.

We fuck for an hour—I'm guessing. It's mostly good. This man, who wants his dick sucked but won't lick pussy, apologizes like a little boy when he says it. He asks, "Should I go?" and buries his head in my shoulder.

I should say yes. I should say that it's terrifying when a man doesn't want to lick your pussy after you've let him fill your throat with his cock. His not wanting to taste me is a banner that I am dirty, that I am not quite wanted, that I am not good enough.

"Hmmm," is all I say because I am already in this. I don't want it ruined. I weigh out the hurts—nothing is so perfect. I take a deep breath and find myself cooing at him, suddenly so young seeming though he is older than me, so ashamed of his not wanting to.

"Can I cum on your tits?"

I sit up on my knees and smile as coquettishly as I can. I bat my too-short eyelashes.

"Maybe we should go into the bathroom" he says breathlessly, as if there is a tsunami of jizz about to wash upon me, as if a quilt is a thing that cannot be cleaned, as if it wouldn't completely ruin and make unsexy everything that has just happened for us to finish our fun in the white too-brightness of a bathroom while I hover in the tub so a man I hardly know can shoot his load on me. I haven't cleaned the bathtub in weeks. It is all I can do to even let him cum now.

"It's fine," I say, stopping short of making that sucking in sound of disapproval between gritted teeth. He stands up on my too-small IKEA bed, and I spread my knees to distribute the weight more evenly. I am willing the slats to hold. He is towering above me, which seems both bizarre and hysterical (the bed being only a foot off the floor so that he could easily stand on the ground and still aim himself at my chest). He uses his hand, I use my hand, I take him in my mouth a few more times, and then he cums.

There is not so much cum. He had over-prepared me. There is some cum, there is *enough* cum, sure, but he didn't need to sound the alarm bells. There is a tiny droplet on the wall and a few more on the comforter but mostly the mark was hit. I am almost disappointed. He is a man who said the world was on fire and then the world wasn't on fire and in that there is a kind of disappointment. He said that he was a hero and he was no hero and after a while a person gets tired of hearing about how they're all such fucking heroes, so goddamn unique and individual, such delicate, little, precious snowflakes just crying out for validation (a validation they themselves so rarely hand out).

Every woman I know has a story about a terrible thing a man has said or done that left her scarred forever. A woman having only one story is a lucky thing. Most of us has stories piled up in every closet of the house. We have to go to container store to find ways to organize all the hurts that men have left at our feet. The time a man told my friend that her lack of tits made her look like a boy haunts her 20 years later as she fucks her husband with her shirt on. The voice of a man who kicked me out of his bed after saying, "I just wanted to see what it was like to fuck a fat girl but I can't," will never leave my ears. I ask a man on a dating app what he's looking for that he hasn't found yet and he says, "A good mouth," and I try not to vomit at the audacity. I bet he keeps big box stores in business with all the women he's damaged. And still, it's men who cry out for validation.

They want to be so special, with their pants around their ankles and their dicks in my mouth and they just want to hear all about how unique and perfect they are, and I just don't have another inch to give. They have made me greedy, or I have decided to be greedy. Either way, I have no more medals to award. I want my own ceremony. I go to the bathroom to get a towel.

In the mirror, I look at my endorphin-full body. Everything seems lighter, just a little bit more relaxed. The bathroom is small, and he doesn't wait for me to finish, so we have to shuffle around each other, changing our shapes like Tetris pieces. I do not ask him to stay because I do not want him to stay.

A week later, when he messages, it has been too many days and the words are too few. I want reassurances of having been spectacular. He offers something else entirely: a mixture of apology and negotiation. He is tepid and meek through implied insults. I can feel his heavy tongue across the Internet.

We're discussing fucking like a workout plan: what I enjoyed, what I'm willing to do more of, where I think I could improve. This is a discussion about me, but I can't find myself anywhere. His body takes up all the room in this conversation. I become a ghost with the outline of his cologne still marking the sheets. This man, who wanted his dick sucked but refused to lick pussy, apologized like a little boy when he said it: asking, "Should I go?" while he buried his head in my shoulder, and I just said, "No, it's okay." Who is this girl that he's talking to? Am I so cheap as to be bought this easily with a meal and an orgasm? When did I become so bargain basement? Who dented my sides, why so discounted?

He made me cum, but I don't feel good. I know feeling good, and this is not that. But it's not immediate, it's not clear exactly why. Because I came. Because I came. Because he made me cum, you see? He took me out to dinner. He was interested and wanted to hear what I had to say. He insisted on dropping me off closer to my door to avoid the rain. He turned me on, we had sex (some of it hot), and then he made me cum, and I woke up brand new.

Now though, *now*, I'm not so sure that his basic decencies balance out the indignities. He wanted to take me to dinner instead of just coffee and I deemed him a prince. I couldn't tell if my value was low or he was just rich with make-believe money.

Now, he suggests a threesome, out of kindness, because I couldn't withstand what he wanted to deliver. I am just a vessel, I think, a sinking submarine. He is shuffling me aside because he wants what he wants when he wants.

I imagine him saying: let's get down to the brass tacks.

We're discussing fucking like a workout plan: what I enjoyed, what I'm willing to do more of, where I think I could improve.

Another week passes, and we barely speak. I hope and I hope, and I hope, but no fix comes. He does not say the words I want to hear, which aren't any of the words they tell you about in rom coms. I don't want him to spend the night, and I don't want him to fall in love. I don't care about romance or love songs. But I am a person, a human fucking person with flaws and an ego, and I want him to have had a taste and want another. Even if the meal isn't on the menu, even if he can't afford the market price, I want his mouth to water.

The only power I have is to disappear. Admittedly, there is pleasure in leaving without explanation, so I delete my dating profile without fanfare. There is no goodbye. I take away the only method of communication. We are lost from each other, or more accurately, I am lost to him. I still check his profile every so often (just to see). I don't know what I'm checking for. And then, three weeks later, at the end of July, I leave Montreal and move back home to Vancouver.

In September, I make another dating profile. I check for him and send a message to say hello. I don't know what I expect—maybe closure, maybe validation—maybe those are the same thing. I expect to be seen as a pest. I imagine that I'm a real bother. I measure out exactly how pathetic I will be, breaking myself against his ribs. But that's not what happens. I say hello, and he gives me everything I had wanted (almost); he gives me everything that I had been too impatient to wait for. He says that he had liked me, that he's terribly sorry if I didn't know that, that he had wanted to see me again, that he had had a great time, that he is sad I'm gone.

He says: I'm sorry if you didn't know that.

He says: Tell me when your book is done, I want to read it.

I say that I will, but I won't. I don't check for his profile anymore. We are lost again.

# LOVE POEMS FOR BUTCHERS

# PERCEIVED ONLINE SLIGHTS

There had been rumors that Tinder wasn't just a hook-up app. I kept hearing about how people were swiping right and then having conversations legitimate enough to lead to first dates, but no one I matched with seemed to believe in being interesting. They all seemed to think themselves hot enough to spark desire without a personality. I spent a lot of time wondering if their parents were ashamed. In the mirror, I examined my own body at length, trying to figure out why they could only ever see a walking vagina.

One man messaged with the singular word, *Anal?*

To which I responded: *only about organizing my closet, but otherwise I'm pretty relaxed.*

*I'm only looking for anal sex*

*Oh thank god you specified.*

I typed it breathlessly, the way it should be read.

He added: *but anything else to…* using both poor grammar and judgement.

*Well don't back peddle now.*

I was genuinely hopeful that he'd get the sentiment as well as the wordplay.
The truth is that he never understands the joke

because he cannot see himself clearly. For today though, the joke is worth it because I can post it on Instagram and make people laugh along with my misery, but tomorrow is uncertain. Tomorrow, someone exactly like him might just crush me. Tomorrow, I might forget that I am more than a sex doll with moving parts.

The next time someone asks what I'm looking for on Tinder, I'm going to tell them the truth: empathy.

Another message reads: *I've masterbated for women before.*

He says this because my bio reads: *Writer. Dater. Masturbator.* He thinks himself witty but when I say it, it rhymes—it's a joke—there's a purpose to the words, accurate but unexpected. When he says it, there is nothing. It's exactly as all the other men before him have said it. He is just another man who thinks he is the first guy to try to talk to me about masturbation. He spells masturbated wrong, even though it says it in my bio, even though spellcheck exists.

*This is super interesting* I type and hope he can hear my eyes rolling back into my head.

*Come over and I can show u*

*Jesus.*

*No, I'm Abraham ;)*

Thank fucking Christ, the man finally gets himself a foothold, and I pray he won't ruin this. I google religious references related to Abraham.

*I Canaan't believe you just said that.*

Maybe he doesn't see the reference or maybe he does and just doesn't like wit. I don't know anymore. I don't anything anymore.

*U do turn me on a lot an r awfully close.*

And then, before I can respond, adds: *I hope you can forgive my horniness ;)*

He says it like anyone doubted whether or not he was sexually attracted to me. He wants forgiveness for being horny, like that was his big mistake.

I write: *did you just use proximity like it was a compliment? Grrrrl you have the prettiest address, so close, so effortless.*

He's thrilled and I'm ready to unmatch.

*Lmao. Ur the smartest woman I have ever met*

I have talked to men who say that women are equally awful on Tinder, but I have a hard time believing them because not a single one has ever been able to provide proof. The kind of man who makes this claim is the same kind of man who abruptly stops talking to a woman he had once conveyed interest in and then, when she's understandably upset and reaching out for closure, calls her a psycho. This is a man who ghosts, one who is engaged in witty banter and then abruptly stops without ever saying a word. This is the kind of man who messages something like: *nice tits!* and then complains about how hard it is to find an intelligent woman, as if he hadn't been the initiator of this kind of tedium.

But I am on Tinder. I remain on Tinder. I am Tindering.

I'm on a hook up app, which I have been told is not just a hook up app, trying to get even just one man to see me as something more than a walking vagina. And that's when I match with Greg.

His name is Greg and we can act like his name is Greg or we can act like his name is not Greg (but his name is Greg), and you have to ask yourself why you assume that a man needs his name changed, why you assume that he will act terribly but also deserves to be protected. You have to ask yourself why Greg is allowed to be anything other than Greg, but I always have to be Victoria. Because I chose to tell the story, I am the villain. Because I am a woman who chose to tell the story, I am a villain. His name is Greg, and so I call him Greg and I write the story as it happened. And I wait for yet another email that reads, "I can't believe you said all those terrible things that were an exact description of how I treated you."

In his pictures, Greg looks fun, though possibly too young (swinging a girl in glow-in-the-dark bracelets over his shoulder on a beach some place like Thailand). His smile is big, and he has lovely teeth. He tells me that he's 6'3", and I can see that he often towers over others in his pictures, which makes me then wonder how short they must be for him to tower so. 6'3" doesn't feel as tall as it used to, and I wonder if my body is revolting against the passage of time by growing instead of shrinking. If online dating has taught me anything, it's that I'm actually 5'10" (and not 5'7" as the facts dictate). Our ages are an inversion of each other; his 23 holds up a mirror to my 32. He doesn't seem to have a problem with it, so I don't have a problem with it—in theory.

Less than a week ago I went out with a twenty-five-year-old, met from the same app, with the same pictures of mine posted, who had rejected me for being fat, which I am, and which all my pictures gloriously convey. We had had a great first date (initiated by him), full of interesting conversation (equally carried by him) that flowed easily. The first time our eyes met though, I could feel that something was off (did I just see disappointment on his face?). I ignored the feeling, thinking myself just a bit insecure and rallied forward. We ended up having great time, full of laughs and interesting conversation, and it seemed like we both had fun playing pool. When it came time to pay and the cashier told us the total for the table, I was shocked at how expensive it was and offered to chip in.

"Would you like me to pay—?"

"Sure," he interrupted.

"—for half?" I said, not even a tiny bit joking.

He let me pay half, which wasn't a great sign but not altogether definitive. Then, while walking me home, he kissed me.

"Would you like to go out again," he asked. "Thursday?"

"Sounds great." I walked home beaming.

The next morning, I received a vaguely hysterical text message saying something akin to: *I can't do this. You're leaving so soon. What's the point? I need to deal with stuff in my own life. I'm busy.*

It looked like a mashup of several excuses people tend to give when bailing out and wasn't entirely surprising given that I couldn't shake that weird feeling I'd had since the first time he saw me. It wasn't long before a couple pointed questions unraveled him. He said that he thought my pretty face and great personality would be enough (to make up for being fat, I guess) but that they weren't. I wasn't sure whether I was more hurt on behalf of—my body (the deterrent) or my personality (never quite miraculous enough). He had used me as an experiment to see if he was a better person than he had suspected, and I didn't need to hear any more of his findings. My fatness was not a crime I had to pay penance for (and, even if it was, I had already paid more than enough).

So, when Greg asks me to go out, I try to push away the memory of this date, still so close in my rear-view. I subdue my trepidation by asking a few awkward questions. Has he looked thoroughly at all my photos? Does he know that I'm a big curvy girl?

I do that. Throw in words like curvy because that's what they call it. That's how they like to describe it, but it's not my word. I would say fat. Big and fat. But they don't like that. Does he like that?

*Of course,* he responds and then adds both kissy and blushing emoji faces. *I look at your pics all the time*, he says, *but sshhh don't tell anyone.*

I wanted to believe he was ashamed purely of the frequency. I agree to go out with him, and we make plans for Thursday night.

*Great.*

*Great.*

Slew of emojis.

The next morning, he texts to say that he had googled me and checked out my Twitter.

*You're actually hilarious, a bit bitter ;) but ur always on point hahahaha.*

I didn't like the way he used the word *actually*. I took issue with his surprise that I was funny and belief that I was bitter.

*So when we seeing each other next, I think I have plans tomorrow night, but Sunday I'm down.*

And because I was free Sunday, we made plans.

The next night, Saturday, he texted: *Missing u tonight babe.*

And then

*Really looking forward to hanging out with u again, we had a great time Thursday.*

And then

*U were super chill and easy to connect with u, I liked it.*

On Sunday night, sitting on my IKEA couch with the bent bar in the middle, he kisses me, and my lip-gloss sticks us together like jam. We make out for a while, and then I break us apart, uncomfortable because of how bright it still is outside.

"Want to watch the stand-up?" I ask, trying to make good on my promise to show him some comedy specials and avoid things going too quickly.

"Naw," he says. "Not yet."

The "yet" catches in my hair like a net. He has a plan. But I also have a plan. I want to get stoned and watch comedy, and then wait till it's dark, like civilized people, to make out and dry hump like grownups and then maybe progress to some in-the-pants stuff.

He stands up in front of me and takes my hand.

"Let's mess around first."

"Let's watch comedy first." (Ooh, our first fight!) It seems weird to me that he wouldn't want to get high first, since we were definitely going to do that, but suddenly I can't remember if I even told him that I had a joint.

"Come on," he says as they always say. The couch creaks as I stand up.

I want to but there's still far too much light pouring into my apartment, everything feels like a casual lunch rather than a midnight escapade. I take a few steps towards the light switch and flick it off, but to my dismay the lighting hardly differs. The sun hasn't set, and the curtain-less windows in my apartment are too big. He sits down on the edge of my bed, atop its magenta pink comforter (which at the moment is no comfort at all), reaching his arms around my body to pull me close to him, and his legs corral me on either side. His height and arms are such that he can reach around my back, while I stand in front of him, to undo my bra. As it falls to the ground, my breasts flop and sag and sway in front of his face.

"Gorgeous," he says, and I'm not sure if he means my breasts, or face, or some combination or even why it matters. I guess it doesn't really matter. We had barely kissed again when he hops up to take off his own pants, which seemed too fast but given the tightness of the pants around his ankles happens slower than you'd expect. I take my jeans off and wait for him to climb back onto the bed with me but after removing his pants he continues straight onto removing his boxers. This time, I do not mimic in kind. Maybe he can sense my hesitation or maybe he'd have gone there next regardless, but he suggests going down on me. Which he then does, for far too short of a time. And that's how it happens then, that this twenty-three-year-old who I hadn't been sure I wanted to do more than make out with gets me naked enough to get laid. Which is exactly, predictably, what happens.

And it is not good.

It's so slow and quiet at times that I wonder if maybe

he's losing his erection (I know I am). There is no energy in anything and whatever connection we have before his dick is inside me fizzles out like a warm soda now that we're fucking (if you can even call it that). At one point, I bring out a vibrator in the hopes of either exciting him, or at the very least, getting myself off. But, I am so thrown by how awful things are going that it does neither. Eventually, I just fake it so things will end and quickly jack him off until he cums. My performance is incredibly lackluster. I'm not sure anyone has ever faked it so poorly. I'm not even sure you could say I faked an orgasm. It would be more accurate to say that I was faking the excitement, the build-up, and when it came time to cum, I just exhaled. His pathetic performance hurt my feelings, assuming of course that I was somehow the reason for its dullness, and as spiteful as it was, I didn't think he deserved the glory of even my fakest orgasm. When it's over, we both dress quickly. I'm already picturing the door closing behind him when he first speaks.

"So, what are we going to watch?" he says, rubbing his hands together, a big smile on his face. He sits himself down in the middle of the couch. I am speechless. Is it possible that he doesn't know how bad the sex was? That seemed too wild to imagine.

But what was I supposed to do now, with this dopey looking boy sitting on my couch ready to watch comedy like he was having the time of his life? I couldn't very well just kick him out (author's note: Yes, you absolute could). The truth was that he seemed so utterly unbothered by the terrible sex that it started to feel like a dream, like maybe it had never happened. Maybe I had made the whole thing up. Maybe I was a time traveler from the past. Maybe the whole thing was a hallucination. Was I having some kind of seizure? The sex was so undeniably awful that denying its awfulness made anything seem possible.

And so, we do what all normal people would do in this situation. We smoke the joint I had gotten from my friend and watch the half-hour special I had already chosen for the night. I want to pretend so badly in the way that he seems to be pretending (or, not pretending at all). He sits so close that again I wonder if we had never even had sex, if it hadn't actually been awful, if there wasn't this weird divide, if I had made it all up.

My eyes burn and an almost comically large cloud of smoke seems to be hovering around my face. The comedy special we watch is one I have seen several times before and yet has never been funnier. I laugh loudly. I laugh so hard it almost hurts. In what seems a manic turn from less than ten minutes prior, I am gloriously stoned and bursting with joy (a small silver lining in this otherwise terrible date). Since we're not speaking, the thoughts in my head have full reign to develop themselves. Am I laughing too much? Am I laughing too loud? Am I laughing during the right parts? Wait, am I the only one laughing? What is laughter? OMG am I even laughing at the punch lines anymore? Does he realize how much I'm laughing? CAN HE HEAR ME?!?! AM I SAYING THIS ALL OUTLOUD?!?! I laugh until I don't even care if he's there anymore. Bizarrely, he stays for another special and then says something about it being late though it isn't very late. I wave from the couch as he leaves, barely looking up. I don't need an insincere kiss goodnight. I can lock the door later.

He doesn't text the next day or the one after. I want him to contact me immediately and also to never hear from him again. There is too much time in the day, and I start to doubt my self-worth, my sexual prowess, my sexual experience, my faith that my woman's body isn't a trash bag of filth. I forget that I am not full of shame. I doubt my decision not to mention that I would be getting my period soon. Likely, soon. Body-so-fucking-unpredictable, soon. I didn't want to bring it up because he's twenty-three and I was already terrified enough about the moment when I would heave my large, sagging breasts from my bra and do twenty-three-year-olds even know about aging and sagging and the inevitable passage of time? Admittedly, he had called them gorgeous. Or did he call me gorgeous? He could see my every aching flaw and scar. Maybe my vagina was too fragrant. Too close to getting my period? Maybe I shouldn't have fucked him? Maybe I shouldn't have let him come over? Maybe I'm over-reacting (hahahahahaha bitch, MAYBE?!?)

A week later, he texts. He is distant and short. He is different. He no longer calls me babe, which had been weird before but now feels hurtful in its absence. He was overzealous then and under-zealous now. I know that we are never going to hang out again, but I ask anyway as a pathway to closure. I want to know why. I want to know if my body is the culprit. I want to know where to place the headstone. I want to know which part of me is to blame.

And so I ask him to hang out again even though I definitely do not want to hang out again.

*Tbh the sex wasn't good for me*

I can barely breathe at the audacity of the *for me*.

*However everything before that was fun. So I don't know what to do ☹ Or what you want*

This isn't enough information though. I need more. I am an addict for the truth, and I have to know where I fucked up or didn't fuck up (maybe I should've fucked down?). I tell him the truth and hope the conversation continues. My heart is thumping in my ears. My cheeks flush but I type with ice cold fingers:

*I'm not really surprised. It wasn't great for me either.*

I don't know what I was expecting him to respond with—humility maybe? Accountability? A division of the blame? At the very least, a question about my experience?

*It was my first time with a big girl so I was a bit off and not used to it.*

His words pound into my back like a thumping fist. They take my breath away. It feels like he's shouting. I can hear him from a mile down the road. His words are so loud I can hear them from the future. Where before, I had thought he might have found my body disgusting for all the regular female possibilities, it turns out that I am yet again segregated. I am not disposable because I am a woman, but because I am a fat woman.

He continues to type: *It's not like I'm not attracted to u, u have a beautiful face and a great personality, I just honestly felt that u were heavier than me and that the sex wasn't at ease really. I was curious, I was down to try something new Iono Hahhaha.*

He says it just like that. Like my size was the problem. Like my body was the disconnect, my shoulders already so heavy with blame. He says *felt heavier* like it's a relative situation, but there was never any doubt that I was heavier. I was heavier in my pictures, and I was heavier on our first date. I was heavier when we played pool. I was heavier when we sat on the park bench and made out. I was heavier when his tongue was in my mouth and his hands were on my breasts, when they moved across my belly. I was heavier when he called me babe and came over and fucked me. I take issue with his use of *Iono*, which I assume is supposed to mean I don't know, and in that he's goddamn right. He has no idea, no fucking clue. I am not a fetish to be experienced. I am not something new he should dabble in. I am a person, though I get tired of having to say the words. I can't help but blame his parents for this. It is exhausting trying to convince men that I am a human being. They chip away at you, a nick here, a crack there. If I ever crumble and turn to dust, I will add water and rebuild again. But you'll still be able to tell. You'll be able to see that I was rebuilt, you will see the put-together cracks, that I was not the original.

*Cool.*

He reads it like a smile, a gentle touch from his mamma who didn't do a good enough of a job, fingers running through his hair. I write it in blood which gets quickly washed away by the tide sweeping the hurts out to sea because if it didn't, I'd never get out of bed again.

*Ya, it was cool. Should we try it again sometime? Maybe if I actually came during sex I would have had a better time.*

He never asks if I came at all. He came during a handjob and now he complains like that wasn't good enough. He never asks if I came. He is unconcerned, completely unaware. He thinks his honesty has redeemed him, as he shifts all the blame onto my weight, as he shifts all the weight of it onto me. He misunderstands that I am trying to end this. He gave me the answers I had asked for and in that, I am grateful. But I would rip off my own skin before I'd ever let him touch me again.

*No, we should definitely not try it again. I do appreciate you being honest about the experience.*

*Ya for sure! Honesty always goes the furthest. Never meant to be mean or wtvr. But I still think we should try it again, to get it out of our system. Lol. U got me fucking down.*

But he is not in my system. I was fucking down when I fucked him and now, I know better. I look at myself in the mirror, sagging tits and all, and remember who the fuck I am. I promise my body I'll treat her better next time. I promise to stop fucking down.

A couple months later, Facebook suggests him as a friend. His profile picture is of him and his new wife. She is rail thin. I wonder if she'll ever get to cum.

# ACKNOWLEDGEMENTS

Thank you to my parents, Gary and Marla Young, for being my greatest supporters. Thank you to anyone who's ever taken the time to read something I've written. These acknowledgements are short but the place in my heart where gratitude goes endless.

VICTORIA YOUNG

# ABOUT THE AUTHOR

Writer. Dater. Masturbator. Victoria Young's work has appeared in *PRISM* magazine and *Cream City Review*. She currently holds two BAs, an MA, and a whole lot of grudges. She was shortlisted for the 2016 Constance Rooke Award. Victoria first rose to "acclaim" as a sex and dating blogger and then later by holding men accountable for their shitty behavior via her Instagram posts. She's a sex positive, angry feminist, and late blooming fat activist who once had a male professor in grad school refer to her writing as Chick Lit without even a hint of awareness. He's probably dead now (fingees crossed).

Made in the USA
Las Vegas, NV
07 January 2022